THE GUIDE TO LUCKNOW

THE GUIDE TO LUCKNOW

CONTAINING
POPULAR PLACES AND BUILDINGS
WORTHY OF A VISIT

WITH
HISTORICAL NOTES ON THE MUTINY OF 1857

M. A. BEG

GYAN

Published by

GYAN

Gyan Publishing House
5, Ansari Road
Daryaganj, New Delhi-110002
Phone: 011-47034999, 9811692060
E-mail: books@gyanbooks.com

Distribution Network
gyanbooks.com
India, USA, Canada, UK, Australia, France

ISBN : 978-81-212-3443-6 (PB)
First Published, Lucknow, 1911

2nd Impression 2020

Printed at: Gyan Press, Delhi.

The Guide to Lucknow
Author: M. A. Beg

THE

Guide to Lucknow,

CONTAINING.

POPULAR PLACES AND BUILDINGS
WORTHY OF A VISIT

WITH

Historical Notes on Mutiny of 1857

SIXTH EDITION.

INTENDED FOR

VISITORS & TOURISTS.

Printed and Published

BY

M. A. Beg.

At the Royal Printing Press,

LUCKNOW.

28th Feb. 1911.

PREFACE.

In putting forward the VI Edition of the Visitor's Guide to Lucknow, the compiler thanks the public for their gracious support and begs to state that great care has been taken in its revision, with all the additions and alterations of the most important nature have been gone into thoroughly and minute descriptions of places of note have been graphically described. The Visitors will find it a ready reference, as all the arragements are quite different from the V. Edition. Nothing in this book has been given by the compiler from his personal information but the whole book comprises of mere selections and compilations from the different Guide Books and Indian Histories of the most recent Publications.

Thanks are due to Mr. G. H. Carlisle Medly, who has kindly revised the book throughout and added the portion regarding the new buildings and road etc.

The compiler earnestly trusts that the Edition under its new arrangements will thoroughly meet the wants and wishers of the Visitors.

THE COMPILER.

CONTENTS.

Historical Account of Lucknow. ... 1

Mutiny at Lucknow. 9

A Short Biography of the Kings of Oudh 16

Guide to Residency 30

Places of Interest at Lucknow ... 47

Lucknow Moharrum 92

Lucknow Bazars 96

New Buildings at Lucknow 99

Lucknow Roads 104

Fountains 106

A

GUIDE TO LUCKNOW.

PART I.

HISTORICAL ACCOUNT OF LUCKNOW.

Lucknow was originally inhabited by Lakshman, the brother of Rama, and was, therefore, occupied by the Brahmans, who were dispossessed by a family of Sheikhs. This family of Sheikhs, who came down with the invading army of Syed Salar (since canonized as Ghazee Mian,) the nephew of Mahmud of Ghuzni, in 1160, A. D , obtained a good deal of influence in the country and consequently supplied more than one member to the list of Subadars. One of their first works was to build a fort, which soon became renowned for its strength. The fort, they built, occupied the site of the present Muchee Bhawun Fort, and is said to have been planned by an Ahir (cowherd) named Likna, after whose name it was called Qilla Likna. Lucknow has derived its name from the two names of Lakshmanpoor and Likna.

When in 1540 A. D. the Emperor Humayon went down to Jaunpore to fight Sher Shah, the then king of Jaunpore, and subsequently Emperor of

Delhi, he retreated, after his defeat, *via* Sultanpore, Lucknow and Philibhit, to Cashmere, and on his way, stopped four hours in Lucknow, where, beaten and dispirited as his force was, and therefore probably, little able to compel obedience, the Sheikhs, nevertheless, collected for him, in that short space of time, Rs. 10,000 in cash and 50 horses. This story proves that Lucknow was then a wealthy and flourishing town.

Oudh was one of the 12 Subas (provinces) into which Akbar Shah had divided the Empire of Hindustan, in 1590 A. D. It was the custom in those times that Subadars (Governors of provinces) had been constantly changed, seldom keeping their place more than 3 or 4 years. Most of them were Delhi favorites, who remained at Court the greater part of the year and then came down to this province, marching about the districts without halts and having collected the revenue to the extent they could recover from the zemindars, they went back again.

When, in 1720, the Emperor Mohamed Shah determined to free himself from the thraldom of the Syeds, he was powerfully aided by Sa'adut Khan, a merchant of Khorasan, who had risen to a military command, and, who, on the successful issue of the conspiracy against the Syeds, was appointed to be the

Governor of Oudh, a position which he retained until his death in 1739. Sa'adut Khan, the progenitor of the Kings of Oudh, lived at Ajodhya and built a fort there. On the death of Sa'adut Khan, his son-in-law and nephew, Munsur Ali Khan, succeeded the Governorship. He followed the policy of his predecessor in keeping up a strong interest at Court and connecting himself closely with the Imperial Government. He was made Vizier, or Minister of State, to the Emperor, in 1747, from which date the title of Subadar ceases, and the Governor of Oudh is called the Nawab Vizier, a combination of two titles of Nawab of Oudh and Vizier of the Empire. Munsoor Ali Khan resided at Fyzabad, of which he was the founder, and which he made his military head-quarters. In his reign the Capital of Oudh was Fyzabad, which place was also retained as the same by Shuja-ud-dowlah who succeeded Munsoor Ali Khan. Shuja-ud-dowlah, in the last years of his reign when Rohilkhand had been subjugated and most of it annexed to Oudh, fixed his residence at Lucknow as being more central. He was succeeded by his son Asuf-ud-dowla, who, at once, transferred the seat of Government to Lucknow, which dates, from this period, its existence as a City and its rank as the Capital of Oudh. Upto this time it was merely a large town of some few hundred houses, extending no further than the area round the Muchhee Bhawun. The site of the Chouk was occupied by a distinct village and the ground, at which the Hussainabad and Kaiser Bagh now stand, was covered with jungie.

From the time of Asuf-ud-dowlah upto the reign of the late king Wajid Ali Shah, Lucknow remained the capital of the kingdom of Oudh. The character and habits of this late king were not such as to encourage the prospect of improvement. Singers and females, provided for his amusement, occupied all his time. They were all *Domes*, the lowest caste in India and they had meddled in all state affairs, and influenced the king's decision in every reference made to him. The revenue was collected by Amils aided by the 80,000 soldiers in the services of Zimindars, of whom half were in the King's pay. The Amils and other public functionaries were men without character, who obtained and retained their positions by court bribery. The revenue was, through oppression, collected from weaks more than what was due, but those that had forts, or by combination could withstand the Amils, made their own arrangements. In this way the revenue was gradually diminished. Numerous dacoities (highway robbery), or other acts of violence attended with loss of life, were annually reported. Neither life nor property was safe. The country was in a state of perpetual unrest and the peaceful inhabitants longed for a change.

The Governor-General, Lord Dalhousie, in 1849, directed Colonel Sleeman, who was Resident at Lucknow from 1849 to 1856, to make a tour through the country, and, after personal inspection, to report upon its actual state. The account furnished by him was a continuous record of crime, misery, and oppression; large tracts of fertile land were over-grown with jungle, the haunts of lawless characters, who levied black mail, at will, on travellers and others. Lord Dalhousie again appointed Colonel (afterwards General Sir James) Outram, Resident in Oudh, to make another thorough enquiry into the condition of the people. His report was also the same as that which had been submitted by his predecessor.

Seeing that it was hopeless to expect reforms from the native ruler, a treaty was proposed to the king by which the Civil and Military authority would be vested in the British Government solely and for ever, under the conditions that the title of King of Oudh would continue to him and his lawful male heirs; that he would be treated with due respect; that he would retain exclusive jurisdiction within the Palace at Lucknow and the Dilkusha and Bibiapur Parks, except as to the infliction of capital punishment; and that he would receive an allowance of twelve lakhs a year for the support of the dignity besides three Lakhs for Palace guards. It was also provided in the treaty that his successors in the title would receive twelve lakhs a year and his collateral relatives would be maintained separately. The king refused, after a consideration of three days, to sign the proposed treaty, upon which refusal the Government formally annexed the province and introduced its own system of administration.

The deposed king was deported to Calcutta, where he was provided with twelve lakhs a year, a separate allowance having been sanctioned for his collateral retations.

Previous to the mutiny Lucknow was one of the most flourishing cities, of great extent and picturesque appearance, in India. The central part of the city was very densely populated; and the scenes in the principal streets were most lively. An intelligent American writer, who visited it in 1856, thus describes the view from the river. "The city, which extends for several miles along the river bank, seemed one mass of majestic buildings of dazzling whiteness, crowned with domes of burnished gold, white scores of minars, many of them very high, lent to the scene that very grace for which they are so famous. The whole picture was like a dream of fairy land. * * * A nearer view of these buildings, however, destroys all the illusion. The 'lamp of truth' burnt but, dimly, for the architects of Lucknow. You find on examination, that the white color of the buildings, which presented in the sunlight the effect of the purest marble, is simply white wash. The material of the buildings themselves is stuccoed brick, and your taste is shocked by the discovery that the gilded domes, of perfect shape and apparently massive construction, which so much attracted your admirations, are mere shells of wood, in many places rotten."

Since the above was written the wave of mutiny has swept over the city. Military and sanitary necessities caused extensive demolitions. The principal buildings still remain, but the chief interest attaches to those which bore the most prominent part in the great siege. The general features of the city have been much altered, and greatly beautified, and no station in the North West can boast finer or better roads, or a more generally inviting appearance in buildings and gardens.

Under the present administration Lucknow is a district in the division of the same name under the jurisdiction of the Lieutenant-Governor of the United Provinces of Agra and Oudh. Area 989 square miles. Population according to the census of 1891, is 7,74,163 being men 4,07,201 and women 3,66,962.

It is situated on both the banks of the river Goomti, which takes its rise in the swamps of Philibhit, on the borders of Oudh, and discharges itself into the Ganges below Benares, the total length being 480 miles and average breadth about 50 yards. In British India Lucknow ranks next to Madras in size and is healthily situated, being 403 feet above the level of the sea. Although it is not the seat of a very flourishing commerce, or manufacture, yet, it is a place of considerable wealth, and the centre of modern Indian life and fashion. Its extreme length, from east to west, is about 6 miles, and breadth 4 miles.

Lucknow is divided into four parts:—The first part comprises the native city, which is extensive but meanly built and squalid in parts remote from the Chowk where everything is bright and cheerful to render it attractive to the gentry who frequent the place The second contains the king's palaces, including the residences of his Court and religious edifices; the third the civil station, which chiefly consists of houses of the European community, and the fourth, the Cantonments, which is separated from the city by the Canal of Nasir-ud-din Haidar. A beautiful panorama of the city and the surrounding country may be obtained from the tops of the Martiniere, Saadut Ali's Tomb, Chutter Munzil, Residency-tower, the Imambara of Ausuf-ud-dowlah and the Clock Tower at Hussainabad.

PART II.

MUTINY AT LUCKNOW.

A couple of months before the outbreak at Meerut, Sir Henry Lawrence (20th March 1857) had assumed the Chief Commissionership of the newly annexed Province of Oudh. The garrison at Lucknow then consisted of the 32nd (British) Regiment, a weak company of European artillery, the 7th Regiment Native Light Cavalry, and the 13th, 48th, and 71st Regiments of Native Infantry. In or near the city were also quartered two regiments of irregular local infantry, together with one regiment of Military Police, one of Oudh irregular cavalry, and two batteries of native artillery. The town thus contained nearly ten Indian soldiers to every European, or 7000 to 750. Symptoms of disaffection occurred as early as the month of

April, when the house of the Surgeon to the 48th was burned down in revenge for a supposed insult to caste. Sir Henry Lawrence immediately took steps to meet the danger by fortifying the Residency and accumulating stores. On the 30th of April, the men of the 7th Oudh Irregulars refused to bite their cartridges, on the ground that they had been greased with cow's fat. They were induced with some difficulty to return to their lines. On the 3rd May, Sir Henry Lawrence resolved to deprive the mutinous regiment of its arms, a step which was effected not without serious delay. On May 12, Sir Henry held a *darbar*, and made an impressive speech in Hindustani, in which he called upon the people to uphold the British Government, as most tolerant to Hindus and Mohamedans alike. Two days earlier, the massacre at Meerut had taken place, and a telegram brought word of the event on the morning after the *darbar*. On the 19th, Sir Henry Lawrence received the supreme military command in Oudh. He immediately fortified the Residency and the Machi Bhawun bringing the ladies and children into the former building. On the night of the 30th May, the expected insurrection broke out at Lucknow. The men of the 71st with a few from the other regiments began to burn the bungalows of their officers and to murder inmates. Prompt action was taken and early next morning the European force attacked dispersed, and followed up for ten miles the retreating mutineers who were joined during the action by the 7th Cavalry. The rebels fled towards Sitapur. Though the city thus remained in the hands of the British, by the 12th of June every other post in Oudh had fallen into the power of the mutineers. The Chief Commissioner still held the cantonments and the two fortified posts at the beginning of June but the symptoms of disaffection in the city and amongst the remaining native troops were unmistakable. In the midst of such a crisis, Sir Henry Lawrence's health unhappy gave way. He delegated his authority to a council of five, presided by Mr. Gubbins, the Financial Commissioner, but shortly after recovered sufficiently to resume the command. On June the 11th, however, the military police and native cavalry broke into open revolt followed on the succeeding morning by the native infantry. On the 20th of June, news of the fall of Cawnpore arrived ; and on the 29th, the enemy, 7000 strong advanced upon Cuinhut, a village on the Fyzabad road, 8 miles from the Residency, Sir Henry Lawrence marched out and gave the enemy battle at that spot. The result proved disastrous to our arms, through the treachery of the Oudh Artillery and a retreat became necessary. The troops fell back on Lucknow, abandoned the Muchi Bhawun, and concentrated all their strength upon the Residency.

The siege of the enclosure began upon July 1st. On the 2nd, Sir Henry Lawrence lay on his bed, a shell entered the room, burst, and wounded him severely. He lingered till the morning of the 4th, and then died in great agony. Major Banks succeeded the civil command, while the military authority developed upon the Brigadier Inglis. On July 20th the enemy made an unsuccessful assault. Next day, Major Banks was shot, and sole command was undertaken by Inglis. On the 10th of August, the mutineers attempted a second assault, which was again unsuccessful. The third assault took place on the 13th; but the enemy were losing heart as they found the small garrison so able to withstand them and the repulse proved comparatively easy. Meanwhile, the British within were dwindling away and eagerly expecting re-inforcements from Cawnpore. On september 5, news of the relieving force under Outram and Havelock reached the garrison by a faithful native messenger. On September 22, the relief arrived at the Alumbagh, a walled garden on the Cawnpore road held by the enemy in force. Havelock stormed the Alumbagh, and on the 25th fought his way with continuous opposition through the narrow lanes of the city. On the 26th, he arrived at the gate of the Residency enclosure, and was welcomed by the gallant defenders within. General Neil fell during the action outside the walls. The sufferings of the beseiged had been very great; but even after the first relief, it became clear that Lucknow could only be temporarily defended till the arrival of futher re-inforcements should allow the garrison to cut its way out. Outram, who had now re-assumed the command which he generously yielded to Havelock during the relief, accordingly fortified an enlarged area of the town, bringing many important outworks within the limits of defence; and the seige began once more till a second relieving party could set the beseiged at liberty. Night and day the enemy kept up a continual firing against our position, while Outram retaliated by frequent sorties. Throughout October, the garrisson continued its gallant defence, and a small party, shut up in the Alumbagh, and cut off unexpectedly from the main body, also contrived to hold good its dangerous post. Meanwhile, Sir Colin Campbell's force had advanced from Cawnpore, and arrived at the Alumbagh on the 10th of November. From the day of his landing at Calcutta, Sir Colin had never ceased in his endeavours to collect an army to relieve Lucknow, by gathering together the liberated Delhi field force and the fresh reinforcements from England. On the 12th, the main body threw itself into the Alumbagh, after a smart skirmish with rebels. Sir Colin next occupied the Dilkusha palace, south-east of the town and then moved against the Martiniere, which the enemy had fortified with guns in position. After carrying that post, he forded the canal and on the 16th attached the Secunder bagh the chief rebel stronghold. The Mutineers, driven to bay, fought desperately for their fortress, but before evening the whole place was in the hands of the British. As soon as Sir Colin Campbell reached the Moti Mahal, on the outskirts of the city proper, General Havelock came out from the Residency to meet him, and the second relief was successfully accomplished. Even now, however, it remained impossible to hold Lucknow, and Sir Colin Campbell determined, before undertaking any further offensive operations, to return to Cawnpore with his army, escorting the civilians, ladies, and children rescued from their long imprisoment in the Residency with the view of forwarding to Calcutta. On the morning of the 20th of November, the troops received orders to march for the Alumbagh, and the Residency the scene of so long stirring a defence, was abandoned, for a while to the rebel army. Before the final departure, Sir Henry Havelock died from an attack of dysentery. He was buried in the Alumbagh, without any monument, a cross on a neighouring tree alone marking for the time his last resting place. Sir James Outram with 3,500 men, held the Alumbagh until the Commander-in-Chief could return to recapture the capital, The rebels used the interval well for the fortification of their stronghold to the utmost extent of their knowledge and power. They surrounded the greater part of the city, for a circuit of 20 miles, with an external line of defences, extending from the Goomty to the canal. An earthen parapet lay behind the canal; a second line of earthworks connected tho Moti Mahal, tho Mess house and the Immambara; while the Kaiser Bagh constituted the rebel citadel. Stockade works and para, pets closed every street: and loop-holes in all the houses afforded an opportunity for defending the passage inch by inch. The computed strength of the insurgents amounted to 30,000 sepoys, together with 50,000 volunteers; and they possessed 100 pieces of of ordnance guns, and mortars. On the 2nd of March 1858, Sir Colin Campbell found himself free enough in the rear to march once more upon Lucknow. He first occupied the Dilkusha, and posted guns to command the Martiniere. On the 5th, Brigadier Franks arrived with 6,000 men, half of thom Gurkhas sent by the Raja of Nepal. Outram's force then crossed the Goomty, and advanced from the direction of Fyzabad, while the main body attacked from the south-east. After a week's hard fighting, from the 9th to the 15th March, the rebels were completely defeated, and their posts captured one by one. Most of the insurgents, however, escaped. As soon as it became clear that, Lucknow had been permanently recovered, and that the enemy as a combined body had ceased to exist, Sir Colin Campbell broke up the British Oudh army, and the work of re-organization began. On the 18th of October 1858, the Governor General and Lady Canning visited Lucknow in state, and found the city already recovering from the devastation to which it had been subjected. (*from a Re-print.*)

PART III.

A SHORT BIOGRAPHY OF THE KINGS OF OUDH.

1. Sa'adut Khan, Burhan-ul-mulk, 1732-1739.

Sa'adat Khan, the progenitor of the kings of Oudh was a merchant of Khorason, who came to Hindustan to seek his fortune. He arrived in Patna, in 1705, a mere lad to join his father and elder brother, who had already proceeded to Delhi, to which place he was obliged to go. He there took up service with the Nawab, which service he soon resigned on being reproved for some trifling fault. Sa'adut Khan then found his way to the Court where he soon acquired favor and made himself a person of importance by aiding the Emperor Mahomed Shah, in 1720, when the latter determined to free himself from the thraldom of the Syuds. Shortly, after this he was appointed Viceroy of Oudh with the title of Sa'adat Khan, a position which he retained until his death in 1739. When he assumed the charge of Oudh, it was in great disorder but he skilfully and ably subdued the refractory spirits and greatly enhanced the revenues. He lived at Ajodhia and built a fort there; he also lived at Lucknow, and changed the name of the fort from *Killa' Likna* to *Muchee Bhawan*, or a fish house, in allusion to the crust of a fish, which he had assumed, and which has since become a decoration on the buildings of Lucknow. Unlike his descendants, who filled the city with palaces, he was content with a comparatively humble dwelling situated behind the Muchee Bhawan, known as the *Pach Mahalla*, for which he paid a monthly rental of 565. In 1739 Sa'adat Khan collected his force and left Oudh to assist the Emperor Mahomed Shah against Nadir Shah. From this expedition he never returned, as he was, it is stated, accused of concerting with Nizam-ul-Mulk, Subadar of Deccan and so he took poison in despair, leaving a large treasure, amounting, it is said, to about nine millions sterling and died at Delhi where he was buried.

2. Mansoor Ali Khan, 1739-1754.

Munsoor Ali Khan, Safdar Jang, was the nephew and son-in-law of Sa'adat Khan, to whom he was succeeded. He also, like his predecessor, kept up a strong interest at Court and connected himself closely with the Imperial Government. He was appointed Vizier, or Minister of State, to the Emperor, in 1747, from which date the title of Subadar ceases, and the Governor of Oudh is called the Nawab Vizier, a combination of the titles of Nawab of Oudh and Vizier of the Empire. He was founder of Fyzabad, where he lived and which he made his military head-quarters. He built the rampart and moat that surrounded the city and had several standing camps near it: so that it can hardly be denied that, in his reign, Fyzadad and not Lucknow, was was the capital of Oudh. He was an able and successful ruler. He died, in 1754, of fever, and his remains were removed to Delhi for interment, where there has been erected over them a grand mausoleum, which is well known as one of the finest structures of the kind at Delhi.

3. SHUJA-UD-DOULAH, 1754-1775.

Munsoor Ali Khan was succeded by his son Shuja-ud-doulah who was appointed Vizier by Shah

Alum. In 1763, when the British quarrelled with their own *eleve*, Meer Cossim, Governor of Bengal, Shuja-ud-daulah took the field in his favor. Defeated by the British, in successive battles at Patna, Buxar, and Calpee, he joined the British Camp and threw himself on the mercy of the victors. It had been intended to deprive him of his territories, but Lord Clive, on a personal interview, reversed the decision and reinstated him on the condition of his paying whole of the expenses of the war.

He made Fyzabad his Capital, which city became a great trade centre. On the last years of his reign when Rohilkhund had been subjugated and most of it annexed to Oudh, he transferred his residence and Court to Lucknow as being more central.

Shuja-ud-doulah was a ruler of great ability and energy, and was, for a great part of his reign, engaged in wars. He is described as being extremely handsome and endowed with great strength. He died suddenly, on 26th January 1775, at Fyzabad, in which city his tomb, named *Gulab Bari*, is one of the chief ornaments.

ASUF-UD-DOWLAH, 1775-1797.

Shuja-ud-dowlah was succeeded by his son Asuf-ud-dowlah, who, at once, transferred the seat of Government from Fyzabad to Lucknow, which has since become a big city and ranked as the Capital of Oudh. On his accession a new treaty was concluded confirming him in possession of Karah and Allahabad, which formed portion of the Oudh Viceroyalty but which were handed over to the Emperor Shah Alum II. for his support. He ceded to the British the Districts of Benares and Jaunpore, worth 75 lacs with a net profit of 25 lacs annually for the better defence of his dominion, stipulating also a yearly payment of £ 312,000 in maintenance of the auxiliary force. He brought about reforms in his army which was put on a more efficient footing by the introduction of European officers into the Military Department. He is held in affectionate rememberance upto the present day, by the natives, who are in the habit of repeating, every morning, this couplet as an auspicious incantation before the commencement of their business—*jis ko na de Maula us ko de Asuf-ud-doulah.*—Whom giveth not *Maula* (God) Him giveth Asuf-ud-dowlah.

Asuf-ud-dowlah presented the doctor with Rs. 25,000 in token of gratitude for the recovery of the kind of England (George III) from a dangerous illness, and at the same time distributed a similar sum in charity for His Majesty's name sake.

Asuf-ud-dowlah encouraged merchants to settle by the widest and most extravagant liberality. He also spent money lavishly on public buildings and gardens, some of which, such as the Dowlat Khana, Romie Darwaza, Bibiapur Kothie etc., are the chief ornaments of Lucknow. He died childless, on the 21st September 1797, and was buried in his own magnificient Imambara at Muchhee Bhawan.

5. VAZIER ALI, 1797-1798.

Vazier Ali, the reputed son of Ausaf-ul-dowlah, succeeded him and reigned for four months, but his proved illegitimacy and worthless character led to his removal by order of Sir John Shore, Governor-General, and the elevation of Sa'adat Ali Khan, the half brother of Ausaf-ud-dowlah and younger son of Shuja-ud-dowlah, who was then living at Benares on a pension of 1½ lacs of rupees. Sa'adat Ali Khan marched to Lucknow where Sir John Shore was encamped at the time. The Governor-General; though was in extreme peril from Vazier Ali's lawless soldiers, yet he, with utmost calmness, maintained his position, and placed the new Nawab on the throne, deporting Vazier Ali, to Benares on the pension of 1½ lacs a year. In 1799, Vazir Ali assassinated Mr. Cherry, the Resident at Benares, who had negotiated the treaty with Sa'adat Ali Khan. He also raised a temporary rebellion, but was defeated taken prisoner and sent to Fort William, where he died in 1817.

What a strange reverse of fortune is that the marriage expense of this deposed king in 1795, amounted to 30 lacs of rupees, while his funeral expenses, in 1817, cost but 70 rupees.

6. SA'ADAT ALI KHAN, 1798-1814.

In 1798, Sa'adat Ali Khan, the half brother of Ausaf-ud-dawlah, succeeded Vazier Ali and earned for himself, during his reign of 16 years, the character of a wise administrator and sagacious ruler. He added the sum of 19,22,362 rupees to the subsidy of 56,77, 668 rupees given to the British Government annually on account of the auxiliary force during his predecessor's reign; and afterwards, for the greater satisfaction of the British Government, ceded to the Honorable E. I. Company, certain district of his dominions which yielded revenue of Rs. 1,35,23,474.

He was a good and just ruler; he had mixed in the society of British officers and had been well trained to habits of business. None of the Oudh Sovereigns conducted the Government with so much ability as he did. He always kept a vigilent eye on the administration, and by a judicious selection of his ministers, the property and tranquility of his dominions were secured. Almost all the pincipal buildings between the Kaiser Bagh and the Dilkusha were built by him.

In the early part of his reign Nawab Sa'adat Ali Khan was given to hard drink, which in a measure tended to unfit him for the duties of sovereignty, but, in 1801, he went to the shride of *Hazrat Abbas*, at Lucknow, where he made solemn vow to abstain from drink and other vices. This vow he kept to the better to the day of his death, which occurred by poisoning, on the night of the 10th July 1814. He was the first man who established a reserve treasury in *A.D.* 1801, and, who, on his death, left fourteen crores of rupees (14 millions sterling) in it. He is buried in the larger of the two tombs on the north east side of the Canning College, while his wife, Khurshaid Zadi, in that of the smaller.

7. GHAZI-UD-DIN HAIDAR, 1814-1827.

In 1814 Ghazi-ud-din Haidar succeeded his father, Sa'adat Ali Khan. On 8th October 1814, Lord Hastings arrived at Cawnpore, where he was interviewed by Ghazi-ud-din Haidar, who returned, after a few days, in company with the Governor-General. In 1819, he received the title of King from the Marquis of Hastings, the then Governor-General, who made him quite independent of the imperial house of Delhi, so that the name of Nawab Vizier now vani shes from history.

It is said that on the day of the king's coronation, jewels and pearls to the value of Rupees thirty thousands were scattered over the heads of the spectators. But the increase of dignity was more than counterbalanced by the degradation to which he was subjected to at hands of his principal wife the Padshah Begum, who was a woman of haughty and imperious character, and whose outbursts often made the king suffer rude rough treatment at her hands.

The former kings of Oudh, fearful of revolutions which might exclude their families from the succession, were in the habit of lending large sums to the East India Company, which, in fact, were thus vested in European securities, the interest on these sums being duly remitted to the appointed heirs. As, for example, Ghazi-ud-din Haider lent to Lord Hastings, in October 1814, for the purposes of the Nepal war, the sum of Rs. 108,50,000, the interest of which, amounting to six lacs and fifty-one thousand, was distributed in the manner described amongst the members of his family.

Ghazi-ud-din Haidar was most polite in his manner, and during his reign no event of any importance took place, Arts and literature were greatly encouraged by this monarch, who died a natural death, on 20th October 1827, and who, according to previous instructions, was buried in the Shah Najuf, on the banks of the Goomtee.

8. Nassir-ud-din Haidar, 1827-1837.

This prince succeeded the throne on the death of his father Ghazi-ud-din Haidar, in 1827.. He married the daughter of the Emperor of Delhi, a very beautiful woman of examplary character, out other wives were soon introduced into the harem, amongst others a woman, of low origin by name Doolaroo who was brought into the palace as wet nurse to the new born prince Munna Jan, whose mother's name was Afzal Mahal. This wet nurse exercised great influence over the king and elevated herself to the position of chief consort under the title of *Malika Zamanee* or queen of the age and at the same time she persuaded him to declare her son, Kywan Jan, who was three year old when she entered the palace, to be his eldest son heir apparent to the throne.

King Nasir-ud-din Haidar was very friendly to Europeans, but not popular among the natives. He led a life of pleasure and debauchery associated himself with companions of the worst and lowest type. His character was undoubtedly built upon the basis of the tutoring he received from the ignorant women and the court eunuchs, decency and propriety with him being at a very low ebb. At times his conduct was very revolting so that the British Resident, Sir John Low, was more than once compelled to decline seeing him or to transact business with his minions. Of the ten crores of rupees left by his father in the reserve treasury, he spent all but 70 lacs. While he was under the state of excessive intoxication, the nobles, dreading his vindictive spirit, had him poisoned on the Light of the 7th July 1837. His remains were interred in the Karbala to the south-east of the Imambara, or tomb of Mulka Afak, wife of Mohomed Ali Shah, situated north of the Goomtee and approached by the road leading over the stone Bridge.

It was in the time of this king that Hakim Mehdi Ali Khan was recalled from Farrukhabad and appointed premier of the kingdom in 1831, in place of the ez-Minister, Aga Meer who left the Capital, in October 1830, with 800 carts and camels and elephants conveying property to the value of 25 crores, for Cawnpore, where he settled and died two years afterwards.

9. Mohamed Ali Shad, 1837—1842.

As Nasir-ud-din Hyder had no legitimate Son, the Padshah Begum, a bold imperious woman who had been living in seclusion at Ilmas Bagh with her grandson, Moona Jan, on hearing the death of the king, forcibly entered the palace with an armed body of retainers and placed Moona Jan on the throne, but, both of them, for this act, were deported to Chunar, where they remained as state Prisoners, in the fort, on a joint monthly pension of Rs. 2,400, which was continued to them upto the moment of their death. After this violent attempt on the part of the Padshah Begum, Naseeh-ud-daula. who took the title of Mohamed Ali Shah, succeeded his nephew Nasir-ud-din Hyder. On his accession he set to work in earnest to improve his kingdom and set right the mismanagement of his predecessor. He has been a sovereign of great ability and experience; and his steady habits and application to business rendered him a favorite with his subject. He died on the 16th May 1842, leaving in the reserved treasury, thirty five lacs of rupees, one hundred and twenty four thousand gold mohurs besides twenty four lacs in Government Security and was buried in the Hussainabad Imambara, which he had built as a burial place for himself.

10. AMJAD ALI SHAH, 1837—1842.

Amjad Ali Shah, succeeded his father in 1842. On his accession, the British Government took the opportunity of pressing the reforms requisite to place the king in a state of tranquillity, for which a limited period was assigned for effecting the change, and, in default of performance, it was intimated that the province would be placed under British management. But the threat proved futile, because, like his predecessors, it was hopeless to expect reforms from a person who passed his time within the walls of his palace, taking no care beyond the gratification of his individual passions, and, therefore, his was an unimportant reign of 6 years. He constructed the metalled road to Cawnpore and built the Huzrutganj, which is now the principal business street in the city. During his reign, likewise, was founded the Aminabad Bazar, so-called after his Minister, Amin-ud-doulah. It is now one of the largest markets of the city. He died on the 13th February 1847 leaving, in the reserved treasury, ninety-two lacs of rupees, one hundred and twenty-four thousand gold mohurs, and twenty-four lacs in Government paper, and was buried in the Mausoleum, which he erected in Huzrutganj as a burial place for himself.

A GUIDE TO LUCKNOW.

WAJID ALI SHAH, 1847-1856.

As Moostapha Ali Khan, the eldest son of the late king was physically unfit to reign, and his claim to the throne was, therefore passed over in favor of his younger brother Wajid Ali, who succeeded to the throne on the death of his father Amjad Ali Shah. His chief architectural work was the Kaiser Bagh, after the completion of which he gave himself up so thoroughly to voluptuousness as to neglect all state matters, and so things were drifted from bad to worse. His misrule resulted in the annexation of the province by the British and he was deported to Calcutta, where he died on the 21st September 1887 in his 68th year.

It was during the reign of this king that the fracas, at Hanooman Gurhi, in Ajodhia, took place. It originated with the Mohomedans, who, under the leadership of one Maulvie Ameer Ali, attacked the local Hindus for the possession of a sacred piece of ground, but they were repulsed by the tact of Raja Maan Singh. The King's troops, sent to quell the disturbance, were also routed by him. This gives another proof of the weakness of the native Government.

PART IV.

GUIDE TO RESIDENCY.

RESIDNCY.

This mansion, now in ruins, and a melancholy monument of the memorable siege of 1857, was originally a very extensive and beautiful three-storied house beautifully built of brick, with lofty rooms, fine verandahs, and splendid porticoes In addition to a ground floor and two upper stories, there were *tykhanas*, or cellar of splendid apartments, as lofty and well arranged as any in the house.

The ruins of the Residency, with the adjoining houses, have been allowed to remain as far as possible in the state in which they were left after "the Relief." The building was built, in 1800, by Nawab Sa'adat Ali Khan, for the British Resident at his court, and it stands on one of the highest spots of ground in Lucknow. The house and gateway at the entrance was the residence of Colonel Baillie, the Commandant at the Military Guard attached to the Residence, hence its name, now identified with many a glorious deed of heroism. Here for five long months a little band of noble hearts held out, with unexampled courage and endurance, against hordes of well-armed, well provisioned, and ferocious enemies All the buildings and in a terribly shatterred state, bearing numerous marks of shot and shell, and every point has a sad story connected with it.

The main entrace of the building was, on the east side, under a handsome portico, which at the commencement of the siege, was barricaded with boxes filled with earth, but the building was entirely unsuited for defence, as it contained numberless, lofty windows which could not be effectually barricaded, the roof being only protected by an open balustrade. On the turret, to the left, was erected a semaphore for telegraphic communication with Muchhee Bhawan Fort, and afterwards with the Commander-in-Chief at Alum Bagh.

The Residency grounds were most tastefully laid out in parterres and contained the choicest flowers and shrubs, which, having been trodden down everywhere, were replaced by piles of shot and shell, and of which there was soon not a vestige left.

The ground floor was occupied by soldiers of Her Majesty's 32nd Regiment, under the Command of Captain Lowe, of the same corps; the rest of the building was filled by officer's ladies and children. In the subterranean rooms (*tykhanas*), on the south side, the women and children of the 32nd Regiment were located. In the upper room, on the south, above the *tykhanas*, Miss Palmer, the daughter of Col. Palmer, 48th N. I., received her mortal wound in the leg, on the 1st July. On the second story, at the east angle of the main building, on the 2nd July, Sir Henry Lawrence received his mortal wound by a shell bursting, and died on the 4th, in Dr. Fayrer's house.

About the 8th August a 24-pound shot, entering the centre room of the building, mortally wounded Ensign. Study, of the 32nd in the arm, and, on 11th of the same month, six men of the same corps, were buried under a part of the north-east wing falling down by the struck of a gust of wind; again, on the 24th, the entire length of the verandah along two stories on the west side fall, burying seven men of the same corps. On this latter date Mr. Ramsay, Assistant in-charge of the telegraph was killed by a shot. The average rate of deaths, for many days, was 20. There were 170 casualities, by the end of July, in the 32nd only.

On the arrival of Sir Colin Campbell's army on the 17th November, the women, children and the sick together with ordnance stores, treasure and State Prisoners were ordered to remove to the Dilkusha encampment, allowing only a certain amount of baggage to each person, and consequently women's apparel, children's clothes, rich dresses, men's clothes, and all kinds of cooking utensils and plated ware bedding and many other valuable things were left behind. Such a scene as that time presented was really sad to behold. Many delicate ladies had to walk 6 miles, over rough ground, especially over the place, between the Motee Mahal and Shah Najaf which was exposed to the fire of the enemy's guns.

In such a way the evacaution of the Residency was effected, after enduring a close siege of 87 days, during which the enemy were always with pistol shot, a further period of 60 days elapsed after the arrival of General Havelock and Outram, when the rebels were driven back on two sides of the position.

BANQUETING HALL.

(General Hospital).

This buiding, which was from the beginning converted into an hospital, was two storied, with very large and lofty rooms on the upper story, standing on the same level with the Residency. There were in the building numerous large doors and windows which suffered much from the bullets and shot of the rebels; the exposed side openings were closed and protected with tents and other materials. On the 8th July the

the Reverend Mr. Polehampton was severely wounded, in one of its rooms, by a rifle ball fired, from Johannes' house, by an African eunuch, who shot many a man in the early days of the siege.

THE TREASURY AND GATEWAY.

The treasury is situated on the right at the entrance into the Residence compound. The treasury and the gateway generally known under the name of Baillie Guard Gate, were garrisoned by the 13th N. I., under the command of Lt. Aitken.

The central long room of the building served as a laboratory for making Enfield cartridges, which Major North, of the relieving force, made from a mould belonging to Lt. Sewell, and a second was found in the garrison.

On the 2nd July the rebels made an assault on the gate but were repulsed; Lt. Graham received a bayonet wound in the groin from one of the Assailants, who was boldly advancing to the very walls. On the 20th August the rebels tried to destroy the gates by fire which was extinguished without causing injury. Subsequently they commenced a mine against this position, but their mine was destroyed by a heavy fall of rain.

Lieutenant Aitken and his men performed good services during the siege.

Dr. FAYRER'S HOUSE.

A very extensive lower-roomed building, with a flat roof, protected all round by sand bags, behind which a steady fire was kept up on the enemy. There was also a large tykhana beneath, which gave shelter to the ladies. This place was held by a party of sepoy pensioners under the command of Captain Watson, Superintendent of the Military Police. It was here that Sir Henry Lawrence died on the 4th July, from the effects of the wound he received in the Residency on the 2nd July. Here also Sir James Outram on his arrival with Havelock's force made his head-quarters.

SAUDERS, (FINANCIAL POST.)

This was a very important post, and was one of the two great objects of the fourth grand attack of the enemy of the 5th September. Between the 1st and 5th the rebels ran three mines in succession against this post, but they were failed in each attempt. The number of mines blown up in front of the Financial Garrison had so broken up the ground as to render this position quite impervious to further assaults of this sort by the time of the first relief.

This post was a large and extensive house of two stories on high ground, being separated, from Dr. Fayrer's house, by a lane, across which was erected a barricade. It was garrisoned by a party of the 32nd Regiment and uncovenanted civilians, under command of Captain Saunders, 41st N. I.

SAGOS' HOUSE.

This house, the property of Mrs. Sago, a school-mistress, was a small lower-roomed, separated by wall from the finacial outpost. This position, commanded by the two 18-pounders and a 9-pounder at the Post Office, and held until ruined on the 14th August, was garrisoned by a party of the 32nd Regiment under command of Lieutenant Clery of the same corps. This was one of the principal point of attack on the 10th August, when the enemy sprang a mine, which fortunately only brought down a few out-houses and two European soldiersthey who were stood sentinel of the out-house picquets were blown into the air, but one at both escaped with their lives. The mining was continued on both sides for three days, till the rebels were blown in and defeated.

GERMONS, (JUDICIAL POST).

This post, which consisted of an extensive upper-roomed house between Anderson's and the Post Office, was garrisoned by uncovenanted civilians (whose families also found shelter here) and the Sikhs of the 13th N. I. under the command of Captain Germon, of the same regiment. This was another important position and was barricaded on all sides with furniture etc. It was much exposed to the fire of the enemy from the east, also from the turret on Johannes' house on the west, only the road side being protected by an earthwork and a wall of fascines. This post, from its being so exposed was completely riddled by the incessant musketry fire of the rebels, who made frequent determined attacks, and was the scene of more hand to hand conflicts than any other post. The enemy tried to blow up the building by mines, but a countermine was sunk, from the well still existing, which resulted in the destruction of about 20 of the rebels.

POST OFFICE.

This important post, which was the head-quarter of the Engineer and Artillery, was defended by a party of the 32n Regiment, under the command of Captain McCabe, of the same corps, who was killed on the 29th September. Its defence consisted of two 18-pounders and a 9-pounder, also two mortars. Here Mrs. Kavanagh had the calf of her leg shot away, but survived. It was here that Major Anderson, the Chief Engineer, died of dysentry, on the 11th August 1857.

There was a workshop attached to it for manufacture of tools, fuses, and filling of shells, during the first siege.

ANDERSON'S POST.

This building which was two-storied, on high ground, was defended by a party of the 32nd uncovenanted civilians, under the command of Captain Anderson, 25th N. I., Assistant Commissioner. It was one of the most exposed outworks in the place; day and night the enemy's heavy gun played on it from 70 to 80 yards distant. On the 20th July, the day of the grant assault on the entrenchment, the enemy advanced in forced this post. They were led by a men carrying a green flag, who was shot and fell into the trench, upon which his followers turned and fled. On the 10th August another attack was made which ended with identical results.

CAWNPORE BATTERY.

This battery which was commenced the early part of June, by Lieutenent J. C. Anderson, and which commanded the Cawnpore Road, hence its name, consisted of three guns garrisoned by a party of the

32nd Regiment, under the command of daily relief of Captains and Captain Radcliffe, 7th Light Cavalry. In this battery were killed, Mr. Bryson, of the Volunteer Cavalry, on the 9th July; Lieutenant Arthur, 7th Light Cavalry, on the 19th and Lieutenant Lewin, of the Artillery, on the 26th. Captain Radcliffe, the commander, died from a severe wound received, on the 25th September.

This battery was much exposed to the enemy's fire from Johannes' house. Many of its defenders were shot daily in their endeavours to keep the enemy out but the flanking fire of the Brigade Mess was of great help to the battery in checking the enemy's attacks.

DUPRAT'S HOUSE.

This house was a lower-storied, with a verandah, having a sloping roof protected by a wall of mud pierced for musketry. It contained three large rooms, with a tykhana beneath, having the same number of rooms. There was another tykhana under the verandah. By the 10th of August this house was nearly ruined by the enemy's incessant fire. The verandah first came down, after which the order wall was demolished. In this house were kept the valuable library of Captain Hayes, and other property belonging to officers.

JAIL.

It was a well ventilated, lofty Barrack, with four equal size compartments and used was a convalescent depot.

MARTINIERE POST.

This building, belonging to a native Banker named Sah Behari Lal, was single-storied with flat roof and good parapet protecting it. It was defended by a party of the 32nd Regiment, masters and students of the College, under the command of Mr. Schilling, Principal of the Martiniere College. On the 10th August, the enemy sprang a mine in front of Johannes' house blowing down the verandah and and outer room of the post, destroying also upwards of 50 feet of palisades and defences. The enemy soon after commanded fire and killed a private, who had accompanied Brigadier Inglis to the scene of the disaster, by a bullet passing through the door-panels. They immediately occupied in force all the buildings round about from which they began a furious fusilade. Several attempts were made by them to get into the Cawnpore Battery, but a steady musketry fire soon made them retreet.

NATIVE HOSPITAL.

Formerly the bullock-train office, consisted of a square of low out-offices. It was situated between the Martiniere post, the Brigade Mess, the Post Office, Civil Dispensary, and Convalescent depot.

BRIGADE MESS.

Or King's Hospital was garrisoned by officers, under the command of Colonel Master, 7th Light Cavalry. It was a lofty double-storied solid masonary structure; its height overlooking all the neighbouring houses. Ladies Inglis and Couper occupied rooms here. Major Francis, 13th N. I., received his death wound, on the 7th July, from a round shot while sitting in the upper story; both his legs were fractured; also Major Bruere, of the same corps, was killed here. On the 20th July, the enemy made a rigorous attack on this building, but they were repulsed, and on the 10th August another similar attack was made preceded by the springing of a mine but were repulsed.

SIKH SQUARE.

This post, which was commanded by Captain Hardings, Oudh Irregular Infantry, consisted of two square enclosures, surrounded by rows of low, flat-roofed buildings, known as Sikh Square, from their being occupied, during the seige, by the Sikh Cavalry. On the 18th of August, a mine was sprung by the enemy, blowing down an out-house at the south-west corner and sending Lieut. Mecham, of the Oudh Irregular Infanty, Captain Orr, of the Military Police, and a drummer into the air; they providentially escaped with but slight injuries.

BEGUM KOTHIE.

The Begum Kothie, previously the dwelling place of the daughter of the grand-daughter of Buksh Ally, whose mother had been a Miss Walters, was one of the largest buildings in the entrenchment and from its structure as well as its being centrally situated, it afforded shelter from the enemy's fire and was occupied by the families of the officers.

GRANT'S BASTION.

So-called after Lieutenant Grant, of the Bombay Amy, one of the Duriabad refugees, who commanded it during the greater part of the siege, and who died from the effects of a wound received by the bursting of a hand-grenade in his hand.

GUBBINS' POST.

This Post which was greatly strengthened and barricaded by Mr. Gubbins jnst before the siege began, and which greatly helped the defenders during the siege, and defended by a party of the 33rd Regiment, Sepoy pensioner, 48th N. I., and Gubbins, Levies under the Successive commands of Captains Forbes and Hawes and Major Apthorp. Many valuable lives were lost in the defence of this post. On the 14th July, the day of an attack, Lieutenant Lester was killed by a matchlock ball; Lieutenant Grant and Capt. Forbes were wounded; and on the 21st of the same month, Major Baks received a bullet through his temples. Dr. Bydon was also wounded at this post on 20th July and Mrs. Dorin, who occupied a room on the north side, was killed by a matchlock ball, on the 22nd of the same month. On the 26th August Lieutenant Webb, of the 32nd, was killed; Captain Fulton, a most destinguished officer, also fell here. Lieutenant Berch, 59th N. I was accidently shot, on the evening of the 2nd September by one of the sentries, who mistook him for an enemy.

The enemy at times made some very determined attacks on this post bringing ladders close up to the walls when they had to be repulsed with hand grenades.

OMMANEY'S HOUSE.

This edifice was extensive and double-storied, and was occupied by Mr. Ommaney, Judicial Commissioner, who was killed in the Redan by a cannon ball on the 5th July 1857. After the death of Mr. Ommaney, Brigadier General Inglis made this his head-quarters, also Sir Henry Havelock and his Staff. The building was fortified by two guns and protected by a deep ditch and hedge of cactus.

CHURCH.

The Church was a Gothic building with numerous pinacles. During the early part of the siege it was used as a store house, but had to be abandoned owing to its extremely exposed position. It was under the cover of this building that the pits were dug, daily in the night, to receive the victims of the day's fire, cholera or small-pox.

SHEEP AND SLAUGHTER HOUSES.

These houses were defended by uncovenanted civilians, under the command of Captain Bolean, 7th Light Cavalry. They were originally the out-houses cook rooms, stables, &c., of the Residency, and were entered through a gateway called the *Ghurrie Durwaza.* The slaughter house was used by the Commissariat Department for the slaughtering of animals for the use of the garrison; and sheep house, as a depot, for the safe custody of sheep preparatory to their removal to the former house.

REDAN BATTERY.

This battery, as one of the best in entrenchment, was garrisoned by a party of the 32nd Regiment under the command of Lt. Sam Lawrence of the same corps. It was erected about the 15th June under the direction of Captain Fulton. It mounted two 18-pounders and a 9-pounder, and was placed so as to sweep the Captain Bazar and the road leading to the Iron Bridge. It was here that Mr. Ommaney was killed by a cannon shot in the head. On the 20th July this position was attacked in force after springing a mine which did no harm, as it had been laid in a wrong direction.

INNES' POST.

This post was a large low-roomed house with a sloping pucca roof having a verandah to the east and north, and consisted of four, large and several small rooms; the central room having a staircase leading to the roof. It was defended by a party of the 32nd, some sepoys of the 13th N. I, and uncovenanted clerks under the command of Lieutenant Longham, 13th N. I., and subsequently Captain Graydon Oudh Irregular Infantry. On the 20th July, the day of the general assualt on the Residency, the enemy made a very rigorous attack on this post, coming close under the walls with scaling ladders, but after several vain attempts were finally repulsed by the hot fire kept on them by the little garrison. On the 10th August another furious assault was made preceded by the explosion of mines, but was as gallantly repulsed.

RESID'NCY LOWER GARDEN.

This was a sort of neutral territory during the siege until occupied again after Havelock's entry. It was abandoned on the first of July as utenable, with tents standing and about 200 unmounted guns of the late king.

On bringing in the ammunition from Muchhee Bhawan, the powder was buried here, but owing to a stack of Bhoosa having caught fire near it, and the enemy occupying the houses on the far side of the garden, it was removed into the Begum Khothie and placed there in the tykhana, heavy beams being laid over the floor to keep it safe.

A GUIDE TO LUCKNOW.

PART V.

—:o:—

PLACES OF INTEREST AT LUCKNOW.

To enable the tourists to identify the edifices described below, it will be necessary to begin from the extreme easterly building and proceed thence, without any deviation, in a westernly direction.

1. BIBIAPUR PALACE.

This palace, situated on the right bank of the Goomtee, is connected by a metalled road with Dilkusha palace, from which it is about a mile distant to the east. It is a doublestoried building and thoroughly English in its style, General Claude Martin being its reputed architect, It was built by Nawab Ausuf-ud-dowlah (1775-1797) as a country residence, where he resorted for the chase, of which he was passionately fond.

It was here that whenever a change of Residents took place, the incoming Resident, or Ambassador, on his first arrival, used to take up his abode, and the following day the Nawab Vizier came, with a large retinue, to welcome and receive the new Ambassador, who was conducted, in great pomp, to the Residency. The procession, with which the Resident was conducted for installation in his new office, was a peculiar scene to the crowds of people who thronged the road, as it consisted of richly caparisoned elephants and horses bedecked with gold and silver trappings.

When it was decided that Vizier Ali, who had been reigning for four months, may be deposed for the proved illegitimacy and the worthless character and Sa'adat Ali Khan may be got seated to the throne, it was in this palace that Sir John Shore, the then Governor-General held a durbar (*levee*) of all the Lucknow nobles and communicated the order of his deposition to Vizier Ali who was afterwards deported to Benares.

The building is now reserved as a convalsecent depot in the hot months for the troops in Cantonments, in the proximity of which, it is conveniently situated.

2. WILAITI BAGH.

Corruptly called *Belati Bagh* to the north-east of the Dilkusha, was laid out by Nasir-ud-din Haider (1827-1837) and planted out with trees of European growth, hence its name. During the reign of Wajid Ali Shah, this garden was in a very flourishing condition, and formed a pleasant retreat for the ladies of the harem, who were entirely screened from observation by the surrounding walls of masonry work that enclosed it on three sides, the fourth, facing the river Goomti, being left open. It is on the banks of the river close to the Dilkusha palace, but there is nothing left to convey the faintest idea of its pristine beauty. Besides the ruins of a summer house, and the graves of a few Britons who fell in the final capture of the city, nothing is to be seen.

3. DILKUSHA PALACE.

The Dilkusha Palace (*literally* heart's delight) was built by Sa'adat Ali Khan as a hunting residence around which he laid out an extensive park and other game.

In 1830, a balloon ascent was made from this garden, by an Englishman, in the presence of king Nasir-ud-din Haider, and a vast assemblage of persons.

On the 14th November 1857, on Sir Colin Campbell's advance from the Alumbagh to the relief of Lucknow, this was the first position assaulted and held in great force by the rebels. After a couple of hour's severe fighting, it was captured by detachments of the 5th Fusiliers, 65th Foot, and 78th Highlanders, under command of Lieut. Col. Hamilton of the last corps. It was here that the relieved garrison on their way to Alumbagh were halted after evacuating the Residency, and that Sir Henry Havelock died on the 24th November 1857.

On the south side of the building, which is now in ruins, are the tombs of Lieut. W. Paul, 4th P. R., Lieut. Charles Keith Dashwood, 18th B. I., and others not named.

For many years after the mutiny, this building was occupied by the General Commanding the Oudh Division, but, subsequently the structure, being considered unsafe, was partially demolished and hence from its present delapidated condition no idea can now be formed of its original grandeur.

The adjoining grounds have. been laid out and tastefully arranged into a flower garden which relieves the gloomy appearance of the building.

4. THE MARTINIERE.

Also called the Mansion of Constantia apparently-ly from the School Motto *Labore et Constantia* inscribed on the front, was built, in the reign of Asuf-ud-dowlah (1775-1797), by General Claude Martin as a residence for himself. When the building was in the course of construction, the Nawab, seeing the elaborateness of the design, expressed a desire to purchase the same, for which he offered a million sterling, but as the king died shortly after, the negotiation was put to an end. The General died before the building was finished and so he directed the completion thereof to be made out of the funds he left to endow a school there.

The building has a very striking appearance especially the central tower which rises from a succession of terraced roofs one over the other, and under which are a series of halls grouped internally so as to produce the most pleasing effects, while their arrangement was at the same time that most suitable to the climate. The central square tower, which rises story to story with four smaller octagonal towers at the angles having winding stairs, is crowned at the top by a dome formed by the intersection of two semicircular arches. On the top of the tower there is a staff for the General's flag, which is displayed on Sundays and other special occasions.

The main building, facing the east stands on a basement of considearble elevation and extent, forming a platform partly paved with stone in front of the entrance hall, and approached in front by a broad staircase and on either side by curved roadways raised between parapets. The wings, which were built after the death of the General, are semicircular of two stories each, the upper stories having arcaded verandahs. An extension of the wings is continued on both sides at right angles to the semicircular portion, and consists of a single story, with arcaded verandahs on the two sides. The two storied front is repeated at the extremities and finished with systyle columns.

General Martin, the founder of the mansion, is buried in a vaulted chamber in the basement eighteen feet below the great tower. The tomb is a simple sarcophagus standing on the floor, and originally had at each angle a grenadier in full uniform standing with hands reversed in an attitude of grief. The figures, executed in brickwork, were destroyed by the rebels, who also dug up the tomb and scattered the bones about, which were afterwards collected and restored to their original resting place. General Martin died at the Farhat Buksh Palace, which was built as his residence, but, according to previous instructions, his body was removed and interred in the Martiniere as a precaution against probable confiscation of the building by native rulers, on a plea of its purchase by Ausuf-ud-dowlah.

In the central vault there is deposited a great bell, which the general had cast in his own foundry, with the superscription on the rim—"Lt.-Colonel Claude Martin 1786" Its dimensions are as follows:—

Diameter of the Bell, 3 feet.
From the crown to the rim 2½ feet.
Circumference about the middle 5 „
Do. of the rim 9 „
Weight about 8,00 lbs.

The vault is well ventilated by means of air-drains which are built in the walls of the tower.

On the west side of the main building there is an ornamental garden cultivated with a number of forest trees and ornamental shrubs, where may be seen a bronze 18-pounder cannon, cast in his foundry 1786, with the words " The Lord Cornwallis "inscribed on it. This cannon was lent by him to the Government of India ; and Lord Cornwallis used it against Seringapatam, in the third Mysore war (A. D, 1790-92), against Tippu Sultan. By the kind permission of Lord Northbrook, Viceroy and Governor General of India, the gun was made over to the

College and now stands in the College garden as a memorial of the founder. The College was established in 1840, and is entirely supported out of the funds bequeathed by General Claude Martin.

To the south, on the road-side, is a low-walled enclosure, within which are the tombs of Captain DaCaste, of the Frozepore Sikhs, and Major Hodson of Hodson's Horse (Captor of the King and Princes of Delhi), both of whom fell in the final assault on Lucknow in March 1858.

Memoir.

General Claude Martin was born at Lyons on the 5th January 1735 and died at Lucknow on the 13th September 1800. He joined the French Army, in his 20th year, as a connon soldier and landed in India under Count de Lally, in the stirring days of 1757. In January 1761 he was taken prisoner by the English at Pondicherry and was sent to Bengal. He, subsequently, entered the English army, and was appointed Captain over a number of his own countrymen. During the reign of Ausuf-ud-dowlah, he attached himself with the approval of the Company, to the Court of Oudh, where he soon obtained complete influence over the Nawab Vizier and became Prime Minister. By his tact and industry he succeeded in amassing a large fortune, but he still remained an officer of the Company, receiving his half pay and promotion to the moment of his death when he was a Major-General of the East India Company.

The reign Ausuf-ud-dowlah (1775-1797), was favorable to foreign art and the General was not slow with opportunity. He built houses, planted parks, cast cannons and commanded patronage. He taught the natives new arts and professions.

He died possessing more than four millions of sicca rupees invested in the Company's 12 per cents, besides large landed property in the province of the Nawab Vizier, in the territories of the East India Company, and also in the kingdom of France. By his Will, after providing for his dependents and leaving large sums of money for charity, he founded Colleges at Lucknow, Calcutta and Lyons.

The motto "*Labore et Constantia*," which is inscribed on the front of the General's Mansion, is characteristic of the energy, enterprise, and indefatigable industry of the venerable adventurer, who commenced his career as a private soldier and died a General.

5. Nasir-ud-din Hyder's Canal.

The project for this canal originated with Raja Bukhtawar Singh, who pursuaded king Nasir-ud-din Haidar, in whose reign it was started, that it would be beneficial to the country to connect the Goomti with the Ganges through a course of some 50 miles with a view of expanding commerce as well as helping the agriculturists, but peculation on the part of both officials and contractors, on one hand and the want of Engineering skill, on the other caused a complete failure.

The canal starts from a bend in the Goomti between the Wingfield Park and the Martiniere Park extending in a south westerly direction for a distance of about two miles close to the Saddar Bazaar, where it curves directly westward for a distance of seven or eight miles near Alamnagar, at which place it was left unfinished.

During the seige of Lucknow, the rebels used this canal as their first line of defence.

6. Wingfield Park.

The above garden, named after the late Chief Commissioner, is beautifully laid out and ornamented with fine trees. In the centre of the garden compound there is an old edifice built of marble stone, within and front to which visitors take seats to receive fresh airs.

7. Hyat Buksh Kothi.

The Hyat Buksh (life-giving) now called the Government House, was built in the time of Nawab Sa'adat Ali Khan (1798-1814) and was originally used by General Martin as his Powder Magazine. After the annexation of the province, it was occupied by Major Banks, Commissioner of Lucknow, who was killed in the Residency and after whom the road at back of the building is named. It is a two-storied house, which is now the residence of His Honor the Lieutenant Governor of the United Provinces Agra and Oudh.

It was within the walls of Hyat Buksh building that Major Hodson, of Hodson's Horse, expired. This position was captured on the 18th March 1858, by General Sir Edward Lugard.

On the advance of Sir Colin Campbell to the Relief of the Residency, this house was captured by Brigade Russel and held during the remainder of the operations by 50 men of the 2nd P. I. under Lt. F Keen.

8. Dar-ul-shafa Kothi.

Dar-ul-Shafa Kothie (house of curing, or Hospital), now forms the residence of the Secretary to His Honor, the Lieutenant Governor during his stay at Lucknow. It was originally constructed and owned by Mr. Joseph Queros, but, after his death in 1822 the building was sold by his heirs, to King Nasir-ud-din Hyder, who, having recovered here from a fit of illness, gave this name.

9. Begum Kothie.

The Begum Kothie, now the General Post Office was the residence of Malka Ahud, Queen of King Amjad Ali Shah. It was erected in 1844. It was here that Major Hodson, a gallant officer, received his death wound. It was stormed on the 11th March 1858, and within two hours from the time the assault began, over 800 of the rebels were killed in the inner court.

10. Kunkerwali Kothie.

This building, is situated opposite to Makbara Amjad Ali Shah and is occupied by the City Magistrate.

Noor Buksh Kothie.

Or Light Giving occupied by the Deputy Commissioner. From the top of this house Sir Henry Havelock, in his advance to the relief, had overlooked the enemy's third line of defences and planed his way into the Kaiser Bagh. The walls of the building, on the west side, for sometime after the mutiny, bore the impress of a shower of grape that was fired at him.

Of the buildings erected by Sa'adat Ali Khan as residences for his sons, this and the above are the only two now existing, others have been demolished ofter the mutiny.

11. Makbara of Amjad Ali Shah.

Commonly known as Chota Imambara, situated opposite the Delhi and London Bank, is the Mausoleum of the fourth King. The building, which is a rectangular structure in the arabesque style, was furnished with costly fittings, all of which were looted by the mutineers; the only ornaments there now are two old pierglasses and a wooden Tazia. A wooden railing about the middle of the centre room indicates the position of the tomb in a vault below. The garden in front the mausoleum is tolerably well kept and the enclosure wall surrounding the quadrangle is built up with numerous stalls, which are occupied by petty traders and artizons, in the north side of which a lofty gateway forms the main entrance.

After the storming of the Begam Kothie, this was the next place taken by Sir Colin, on the 14th March 1858, after a severe struggle.

The Memorial in front of the East Gate of the Kaiser Bagh.

The Memorial, erected at the space in front of the East Gate of the Kaiser Bagh, between it and the Tarawali Kothie, commemorates the massacres, on the spot, on the 24th September and 16th November 1857, of the two separate parties of European captives, one consisting of those sent in by the Dhowrera Raja (Miss Jackson, Mrs. Green, Mrs. Rogers, Mr. Carew, and Mr. J. Sulivan) with the addition of some persons captured in the town, deserters from the Bailey Guard; and the other consisting of the victims of the Mithowlie Raja's gratitude and hospitality (Sir Mountstuart Jackson, Capt. Orr. Lt. Burns, and Sergeant Morton).

On the first day of October 1859, Raja Jialal Singh, a man of large territorial possessions and of great influence with the mutineers, was executed on this very spot, where he had committed the crime. He was one of the leaders of the rebellion, who followed the first party of prisoners to the fatal scene, and mounted one of the gates (since demolished) of the Kaiser Bagh, in order better to feast his eyes on their dying agonies, and to applaud of his sepoys.

13. Tomb of King Sa'adat Ali Khan.

Within the enclosure of the Kaisar Bagh, close to the Canning College, (no Museum) on the north-east side there stand the two tombs of Sa'adat Ali Khan (called after his death Jannat Aramgah, or one whose soul is in paradise) and of his wife Khurshaid Zadi (daughter of the sun.) Both these tombs were built by Ghazi-ud-din Haidar after the death of his parents. By this construction he displayed a very uncommon amount of filial affection, as on the spot on which his father's tomb now stands, formerly stood the house in which he lived himself during the life-time of Sa'adat Ali Khan, and it is said that, when he succeeded the throne and occupied Sa'adat Ali Khan's place, fully appreciating the charge in their respective situations, he remarked that, as he had now taken the house of his father, it would be nothing but right to give up his own to his father. Accordingly he ordered to destroy his former abode, and to build, on the site, a tomb to his father.

During the advance of General Havelock's relieving force to the Residency; they were greatly harassed by the rebels's destructive fire at this point as they held the position in great force the tops of the tombs giving them material advantage.

The tombs have winding stairs and the ground surrounding them is beautifully adorned with green grass and iron railings.

15. The Canning College.

The Canning College which is now removed to a new building espically built for the College was established in 1864, is principally intended for the education of the sons of the native nobility by whom the institution is mainly supported. Now it is a College comprising only the classes above the Entrance Class, as the stndents upto Entrance class are taught in the Jubilee High School opposite to R. & K. Railway station and the sons of Taluqdars are brought up in the Colvin School lately established in the newly built edifices across the river.

The Canning College is governed by a committee under the presidentship of the Commissoner of Lucknow. The present building which the college occupies, is situated within the enclosure of the Kaiser Bagh, and was completed in 1878.

A GUIDE TO LUCKNOW.

THE KAISER BAGH.

This building, which is the largest, grandiost and most debased of all the Lucknow palaces, was built by Wajid Ali Shah, the last king of Oudh between 1848-1850 costing about 80 lacs (£ 800,000) including furniture and decorations. It consists of a great square of buildings with a very large court yards and four gateways, one of which has since been demolished. Entering by the north-east gateway, which faces the open space in front of the observatory, or Tarawali Kothie the visitor would pass through a court to a gate known as the Jiloukhana, (since demolished) from where the royal procession used to start. Turning to the right, through a screened gatoway, he would arrive at the Chini Bagh, so called from the china vessols which formerly decorated the gardens. On the right hand there lie the Chandiwali Baradari (once paved with silver) built of stone of picturesque design, and the Khas Mukam as well as the Badshah Munzil, the special residence of the King, erected by Sa'adat Ali Khan, but included by Wajid Ali Shah in the plan of his new palace. Nawab Ali Naki Khan, the Vizier (minister) of the king, used to live above the mermaid gateway so that he might be close at hand to attend any summons from the King. On the left hand side there stands a large confused pile of buildings, called the Chaulakhi, which was built by the King's barber, Azimulla Khan who subsequently sold them to the king for four lacs, hence so-called. It formed the residence of the Queen and the chief concubines; and here the rebel Begum held her court while the British prisoners lay, for weeks, in one of the adjacent stables. The roadway proceeds past a large mulberry tree (since fell) which was paved round the roots with marble and under the whodas of which the King Wajid Ali, used to sit dressed in the yellow robes of a fakir, (an oriental ascetic or begging monk), on the occasion of a great fair called the *Jogia Mela*) held in the month of August, within the Kaiser Bagh square, to which all dressed in the garb of a fakir were admitted. The eastern Lakhi gate, called from its having been built at a cost of one lac of rupees, gives access to a magnificent open square, known pre-eminently as the Kaiser Bagh. The Stone Baradari, situated in the centre of the quadrangle, is now the property of Maharani Bulrampore.

The buildings forming the quadrangle of the Kaiser Bagh are mostly double-storied but various in design several of which contain large and handsome halls. They are occupied by the Talukdars (landed proprietors, or Barons of Oudh) for their periodical visits to Lucknow, as the same have been made over to them for this purpose. It is in this building that fetes take place in honor of the arrival of any new Lieutenant Governor, Viceroy, or other exalted personage, whose visit to the Capital is blazoned throughout the land by a grand illumination and a great pyrotechnic display which the public are permitted to witness. Admission, however, to the Baradari, where refreshments are provided, is given by tickets issued to those for whom the place is reserved.

KAISAR PASAND.

Passing by the western Lakhi gate of Kaiser Bagh, we have, on our left, the building known as the Kaiser Pasand of Caesar's choice (now the Deputy Commissioner's Court). This building which is also called *Roshan-un-dowlah ki Kothi*, was erected by Roshan-ud-dowlah, Prime Minister of Nasir-ud-din Haider; but Wajid Ali Shah confiscated it and gave it as a residence to his favorite concubine Mashuk-ul-Sultan. In the under stories of the building were confined the Dhowrera party of European captives, who were killed on the spot marked by the memorial in front of the Kaiser Bagh gate.

Sher Darwaza.

Or Neill's Gateway, adjacent to which has lately been erected masonry pillar, beaing a stone slab, which marks the spot where fell General Neil, whose remains were interred in the Residency Cemetery.

Chutter Munzil Palaces.

Chutter Munzil is a term properly applied to those buildings Surmounted with a "Chutter," or gilt Umbrella; of these are two; the (1) *Greater Chutter Munzil*, which is at present occupied by the United Service Club, is a three storied building having tykhanas or underground rooms. It was built as a residence for the ladies of the harem by Nasir-ud-din Haider, who himself occupying the adjoinin galace pcalled the Farhat Buksh. The (2) *Lesser Chutter Munzil* is a two-storied building surmounted by a dome with a gilt Umbrella, and is now occupied by Office of the Department of Land Record and Agriculture United Province of Agra and Oudh. The two buildings immediately behind it facing the road leading to the Residency are the *Gulshan-i-aram* (Heavenly Garden), in the under-ground rooms of which, it is said that King Nasir-ud-din Haider was poisoned, and *Darshanbilas* (pleasing vision) also known as the "*Chowrukhi Kothie*" a designation it derives from each of its four sides representing the facade of four different edifices. The *Gulshan-i-aram* was formerly used for a part of Museum but now it is occupied by some Govt. office a part of the Museum and office of the Curator, while the *Darshani-bilas* is occupied by the office of the Inspector of Schools and Pubic Works Department.

Between the above two Chutter Munzils there was a very pretty garden with a beautiful marble tank in the centre of which was an island covered with a pavilion.

On the 6th October 1891, when the flood was much higher than that of 1870, the Gomtee rose level with the plinth of the *Greater Chutter Munzil* and threatened to surmount the stone platform when it would have been into the club rooms and the rooms of the adjoining building containing the Library, at the north corner of which last (the ground here being low) a bund, or barrior, was hurriedly constructed across three doors to keep out the water.

This *Greater Chutter Munzil* was stubornly defended by the mutineers till driven out by the relieving force of General Havelock on the 25th September 1857.

Furhat Buksh.

The Furhat Buksh (giver of delight) palace together with the adjoining building formed the principal residence of the Oudh Sovereigns from the time of Sa'adat Ali Khan until Wajid Ali Shah built the

Kaiser Bagh. It originally formed the residence of General Claude Martin, by whom the palace was built and afterwards sold to Nawab Asuf-ud-dowlah. Sa'adat Ali Khan made great additions and improvements to the place.

These palaces were held in great force during the advance of General Havelock's relieving force, who had to cut their way through a murderous fire, on the 25th September 1857, losing heavily.

The Lall Baradari.

Or Throne room, so named on account of the building being painted inside and out with red ochre, was originally set apart for Royal Durbars. On the day of the accession of a new King it was customary for the Resident to place him on the throne and present him with a Nazar (offering) in token that the British Authority confirmed his assumption or the Government.

It was here that, after the death of Nasir-ud-din Haidar, the attempt on the throne by the Padshah Begum and Moonna Jan took place and in pursuance of the custom mentioned above the insurgents attempted to force the Resident, Colonel Low, to present an offering to Moonna Jan, as he sat on the throne, thinking thus to confirm the usurper's authority. The Resident was nearly killed in this place for setting aside the claim of Moonna Jan to the throne in favor Mohomed Ali Shah, the uncle of Nasir-ud-Haidar.

The Residency.

This mansion, now in ruins and a melancholy monument of the memorable seige, was built, in, 1800, by Nawab Sa'adat Ali Khan, for the British Resident at his court. It stands on an elevated spot not far from the Chutter Munzil. It was originally a very extensive and beautiful brick building consisting of lofty rooms, fine verandahs, and splendid porticoes. Besides having a ground floor and two upper stories, it had *tykhana*, or cellar of splendid apartments, as lofty and well arranged as any in the house. This house, during the time of trouble, afforded accommodation to very numerous families. For detailed description of the intrenched position see Part III.

Muchee Bhawun.

This was the name of the fort (since demolished) originally called Qilla Likhna after a Hindu cowherd called Likhna and changed to Muchhee Bhawan by Sa'adat Khan on his assuming the crest of a fish as an emblem of Royalty. It comprised a much larger area than that which was contained within the limits of the old fort of that name which was surrounded by high walls, the side towards the river having the appearance of a castle. Towards the river front the fortifications commanded the stone and iron bridges; the south and west had been one of the most populous parts of the town, which, being partially levelled at the time of the mutiny; towards the least, fort commanded the Residency and overlooked some very frequented thoroughfares.

The high ground on the river side, crowned by the Mosque built by Aurangzeb of Delhi, Lukshman Tela, the site of the original Lukshmanpore. Backwards of the Muchee Bhawan itself, in a southernly direction, is an open space, once a depot for ordnance stores, that marks the site of Mobarak Mahalls and Pach Mahalla (now demolished), the oldest houses in Lucknow, built by the family of Sheikhs who formerly owned territory here.

The buildings in the Muchhee Bhawun belonged to Nawab Yahya Ali Khan, who sold them to Sir Henry Lawrence for Rs. 50,000. These buildings originally formed the stronghold of the ancient Sheikhs, who became so troublesome in the time of Ausuf-ud-dowlah, as to incur the displeasure of the

Nawab who confiscated the property, when he removed his capital from Fyzabad to Lucknow.

At the time of the outbreak of the mutiny in Oudh this was considerably strengthened by Sir Henry Lawrence with the view of standing a siege, but after some time it was abondoned on the 2nd of July 1857, by the garrison who retreated to the Residency with such guns, ammunitions etc. as was feasible. The remainder of the material which could not be removed was blown up.

After the re-occupation of Lucknow, this fort was rebuilt, stongly fortified and re-garrisoned, but on completion of Redoubt No. 1, in Dilkusha Contonments, the fortification was completely demolished and the great Imambara of Asuf-ud-dowlah and its adjoining Mosque, made over the Mohomedans, who were greatly gratified at the concession on the part of the British Government.

THE GREAT IMAMBARA.

Within the precincts of the Muchee Bhawun is the Great Imambara (House of the Prophet) which is the architectural gem of Lucknow and the crowning work of the reign of Nawab Ausuf-ud-dowlah who is said to have spent incredible sums on it. The natives report that the building cost a million sterling (one crore of rupees). Nawab Ausuf-ud-dowlah invited architects to submit their plans to competition as he wished that the building should be no copy of any other work, and that it should surpass, in beauty and magnificence, anything of the kind ever built by his predecessors. Kifayet-Ullah was, however, the successful competitor, and the imposing edifice, as it stands, is a proof that his conception answered the King's ostentatious requirement.

This superb edifice, together with the Romie Darwaza hereinafter described, was started as a relief work during the terrible famine which raged from 1784 to 1786. In the middle of the central hall are interred the remains of the late Nawab Vizier who died in 1797.

Excepting the galleries in the interior no wood work has been used in the construction of this Imambara. The main room is reputed to be the largest vaulted hall in the world, its dimensions are as follows:—

CENTRE ROOM.

Length within, ...	163 feet.
Breadth of room, ...	53 ,,
Height	49½ ,,
Intrados, or inner line of arched roof	68 ,,
Thickness of walls	16 ,,

A GUIDE TO LUCKNOW.

Octagonal Room—East.

Circumference	...	...	...	216 feet.
Height,	...	...	...	53 „
Thickness of wall		...	...	16 „

Square Room—West.

Square,	...	...	...	54×54 feet.
Height	...	...	...	53 „
Thickness of walls,		...	...	16 „

Extreme Measurement of Building.

Length,	...	...	...	303 feet.
Breadth,	...	...	...	163 „
Height,	...	...	...	63 „

There is a splendid Mosque adjoining the Imambara with minarets on either side from the summit of which a grand panoramic view is obtained of the city and surrounding buildings. During the Moharram festival the whole building is illuminted nightly, one night only, the 6th, being set apart for European visitors also at the Shah Najuf and Hussainabad.

ROMIE DARWAZA.

Or Turkish Gate, is the western gate of the enclosure of the Imambara. It is a structure of massive proportions faced, on both sides, with some imitation of leaves which rise from the base and radiate above the spring line forming a pointed arch. The arch-way is surmounted by a turret which completes the design. This gate is supposed to be a fascimile of one of the gates of Constantinpole, but persons who have visited that city declare that there is no gate standing there now which at all corresponds with this one, and the only inference to be drawn is that the Nawab Vizier was probably the victim of a deception.

HUSSAINABAD CLOCK TOWER.

This tower, which is of recent date (1881), was erected from the design of Mr. R. R. Bayne, of Calcutta, for the reception of a clock of great size and power, made by Mr. J. W. Benson, Ludgate Hill, London, by the trustees of the Hussainabad Edowment who administer a fortune of some 36 lacs of rupees bequeathed by Mohumed Ali Shah. It was taken in hand at the suggestion and through the influence of the City Magistrate, Lieutenant-Colonel Norman Horsford, Bengal Staff Corps. It has a very stately appearance, the tower being 221 feet high and 20 feet square.

The following are the weights and notes of the bells:—

	Weight.			Note.
	Cwt.	Qr.	lb.	
Hour bell	20	2	0	Eb.
Fourth quarter	8	3	11	Bb.
Third „	8	0	12	E.
Second „	6	0	12	F.
First „	5	3	0	G.

This is by far the largest clock in India.

THE HUSSAINABAD TANK.

Along with the Hussainabad Imambara, to be hereafter described, this magnificent pucca tank, which is contiguous to the Clock Tower, was built by Mohomed Ali Shah. It is well stocked with fish and is supposed to have an underground connection with the river.

The Sat Khunda.

Or Seven-storied, having been originally designed as such, stands at west of the Husainabad Tank in an unfinished circular tower. It was commenced by Mohomed Ali Shah for a watch-tower, from whence he might survey the extent and magnificence of his palatial domain, but the tower only reached its fourth story when the King died and the work was stopped

Dowlut Khana.

Literally the residence of a superior, or great man, is the old palace of Ausuf-ud-dowlah after the transfer of the seat of Government from Fyzabad to Lucknow, in which are included a number of other buildings. It was relinquished by Sa'adat Ali Khan who transferred his Court to the Furhat Buksh. The Dowlat Khana is now occupied by a wealthy Nawab, who is said to be in some way connected with the Royal family of Oudh.

The Baradari opposite the tank was erected by Mohomed Ali Shah, and has recently been repaired and improved at a great cost. This building is now used as a place of conference for the native nobility and also as a picture gallery, or repository for the portraits of all the Kings of Oudh, which were formerly kept in one of the side rooms of the Imambara of Hussainabad.

The Hussainabad Imambara.

This is the only architectural work of Mohomed Ali Shah, the third King of Oudh. It is an oblong building divided into three rooms with smaller compartments at the ends. The partition walls are profusely ornamented in Arabesque, and the central room contains the tombs of both the King and his mother The roof is vaulted throughout, and over the centre is a gilded dome. The floor is paved with black and white marble artistically arranged. The garden, which occupies the quadrangle, is somewhat disfigured by being crowded with a bad model of the Taj of Agra on the west, (in which is buried the King's daugher) and, on the east there is a building of similar dimensions. On the right of the Taj is a small mosque for the exclusive use of the surviving heirs and successors of departed royalty. A lofty gateway of three pointed arches, richly wrought in stucco, in a northern side of the large quadrangle, forms the main entrance to the Imambara.

A well-appointed establishment is employed to keep up the splendour of the Imambara, and the expenses are defrayed from a large fund allotted, in the lifetime of the King, for the purpose. The annual illuminations, on the anniversary of the King's death and for several nights during the Moharrum Festival, make this quarter a great centre of attraction to the populace, one night is specially set apart for European visitors, same as at the Great Imambara and the Shah Najuf.

Jumma Musjid.

So-called from its being chiefly used on Friday (*Jumma*), as the place of worship by the Mohomedans. This is the great mosque of the city, situated west of the Hussainabad Imambara, and like all other mosques, constructed with two minarets and three domes, the largest one being in the middle. It was commenced by Mohomed Ali Shah, and intended to surpass the mosque of Ausuf-ud-dowlah in the Muchee Bhawan, but the King died before its completion. It was, however, resumed and completed by Begum Mulka Jehan, a surviving member of the royal family, who is now dead.

The edifice stands on an elevated basement with an open platform in front, fitted with lavatories for the use of the worshippers, The floor is a marble pavement and the walls are beautifully ornamented, with the arches colored in stucco

Moosah Bagh.

Far beyond the Husainabad, in a northerly direction, is this garden, within a high-walled enclosure, comprising an area of seven or eight acres, and remarkable for its elevation above the surrounding level, especially towards the river. It was laid out as a garden by Ausuf-ud-dowlah, but the house was built by Sa'adat Ali Khan, who made it his favorite country residence About three hundred yards to the north of it flows the Goomty, whose opposite bank is said to have been the scene of many a fight of wild beasts, which were witnessed by the Vizier and his courtiers from the above palace The building is in the English style, and is said to have been designed and constructed by General Martin. Within the garden is a low-walled enclosure, containing the tomb of Captain. T. Wale, who raised and commanded the 1st Sikh Irregular Cavalry, killed in action on the 21st March 1858, evidently when in pursuit of the flying enemy.

This was the last position held in force by the rebels in the final capture of the city. It was captured by General Outram on tho 19th of March 1858. The enemy had, it is said, 6,000 men and thirteen guns here. When the troops approached the garden, the enemy opened with their guns; their fire was immediately replied to by Capt. Middleton's Royal Light Field Battery. The 79th Highlanders and 23rd Fusiliers were thrown out in the wood to the right and left in skirmishing order, the 9th Lancers making a flank movement to the left; the enemy, after a short resistance, abandoned their position and fled. They were pursued for six miles and all their guns were captured.

Badshah Bagh.

The road over Bruce's Bridge, east of the Chutter Munztl, leads into the Badshah Bagh, which is a garden of great extent surrounded by high walls. It is entered on three sides by lofty gateways and was a Royal Garden laid out by Nasir-ud-din Haidar In the centre of this garden there is a substantial stone edifice partly two storied, with an open arcaded hall at the back, its front has round towers at the angles and faces south. The edifice is well adapted for festive gatherings (such as picnics, etc.) allowed to be held here by the kind permission of His Highness, the Maharaja of Kapurthala, to whom the property now belongs. There is also north of the building a large masonry tank, spanned about the centre by an iron bridge and rounded with gravel walks. On the left of the garden, which is planted with numerous fruit trees and ornamental shrubs, is a large building which was sacred to the ladies of the King's harem.

Moti Mahal.

Or Pearl Palace, built by Sa'adut Ali Khan, lies on the right bank of the Goomti, a little above the Shah Najuf. The Moti Mahal, so-named after a favorite Begum of the King, includes three separately named and distinctly buildings now the property of the Maharani of Bulrampore. It was built by Sa'adut Ali Khan (1798-1814) and forms the northern part of the enclosure, which contains the Mobarrak Munzil and Shah Munzil, or royal hall built along the river face by Ghazi-ud-Haidar. It was within the enclosure of this building the combats between tigers, etc. was held. The encounter between the elephant and rhinoceros, which required to be viewed at a safe distance, took place across the river on the ground in front of the Hazri Bagh, the building now occupied by the Oudh Ice Company, the King and his court watching it from the verandah of the Shah Munzil.

It was in the courtyard of Moti Mahal the Brigadier Cooper Commanding the Artillery and Bartram were killed, as also Captain Crump, of Madras Artillery, Colonel Campbell, Commanding Her Majesty's 90th, were mortally wounded. This place was the advanced position taken by Sir Colin Campell's relieving army; and it was here that the rear guard, and heavy guns and wounded men of General Havelock's force halted on the night of the 25th September 1857. At the gateway one of General Havelock's 24-pounders stuck on the 25th September.

Khurshaid Munzil.

Or Happy Palace, struck by lightning on the evening of 12th March 1891, without injury to life or property, was named after Khurshaid Zadi, the wife of Nawab Sa'adat Ali Khan, who began the construction of the edifice, which which was completed by his son Ghazi-ud-din Haidar. It is built in the form of a castle, and is surrounded by a moat 12 ft. broad, over which there was formerly a draw bridge, but this has since been replaced by a masonry bridge (or bridges, since there are now four entrances), by which access is gained to the building.

This handsome and commodious double-storied building is now the property of the Lucknow Martiniere Girls School, to whom it was made over as a free gift by Government on the 27th November 1876. Extensive additions and alterations have been made to the building which is now admirably suited to the requirements of a Boarding School by the expenditure thereon of more than sixty thousand rupees from the Martiniere "Female Education Fund."

After the annexation, it was used as the Mess House of the officers of the 32nd Regiment. It was stormed by Sir Colin Campbell's relieving force and shortly after its capture Sir Colin was met by Generals Outram and Havelock.

Tarawalie Kothie.

Or observatory, now occupied by the (Bank of Bengal) was built in the reign of Nasir-ud-din Haidar, under the supervision of Colonel Wilcox, Astronomer Royal to the King, who had it fitted with the necessary astronomical instruments.

The Colonel died in 1847, and Wajid Ali Shah abolished the department and the instruments were put by, but they were all destroyed in the mutiny. During the mutiny the Fyzabad Moulvie Ahmadulla Shah made this his head-quarters, and the rebels frequently held their meetings here.

Shah Najuf.

Otherwise called Najuf Ashraf, is situated on the right bank of the Goomti close to the Horticultural gardens, built as a mausoleum by Ghazi-ud-din Haidar, who is buried therein with his wife and other members of the royal family. It is illuminated during the Moharram Festival and on the anniversary of the King's death, at the expenses defrayed out of the sum endowed by the King for this purpose and for the maintenance of an establishment to look after it. On these occasions this mausoleum is visited by great crowds of all classes; European visitors being admitted until midnight on the 6th Moharram.

The building is in the form of a square measuring about 40' × 40' in the interior and is roofed by a single dome. The floor is tessalated pavement of marble, the walls adorned with drawings by native artists and is furnished with pier glasses and chandelier.

Kadam Rasul.

Or the Prophet's foot-print, was a Mohomedan place of worship built in the time of Nasir-ud-din Haidar (1827-1837) on an artificial mound of earth to the east of the Shah Najuf. It contained a stone which is said to bear the impress of a foot of the Prophet, brought by a pilgrim, from Arabia, as a sacred relic. The stone was carried of during the mutiny and has not since been recovered. The building is falling into decay and is no longer a place of veneration.

Secunder Bagh.

Or Alexander's garden, was built by Wajid Ali Shah (1847-1856) and given by him to one of his wives Secunder Mahal, from whom it derives its name. It is a quadrangle enclosure (about 150 yards square) with turrets at the angles, and originally contained a garden, prettily laid out with a summer house in the centre, which is still standing. Intrinsically there is nothing now in the place deserving of notice; its fame arises from the tremendous retribution that here overtook the rebel sepoys on the 16th November 1857, at the final relief of Lucknow.

"On the head of the attacking column advancing towards it, a severe fire was poured into them; the Infantry of the column were thrown into skirmishing order and directed to line a bank to the right of it, whilst Captain Blunt's troop of Horse Artillery, and Captain Traver's Royal Light Field Battery, dashed to the point at a gallop, through a cross fire from a village and the Secunder Bagh, and opening fire upon it within easy musket range in a most daring manner. Two 18-pounders were also brought to bear on it; and after an hour and a half's pounding, a small breach was made, through which the 93rd foot and 4th Punjab Rifles dashed. Never was a bolder feat of arms done. The rebels inside made a desperate resistance, and were all cut to pieces; upwards of 2,000 bodies were carried out and buried. The slain were all sepoys of different mutineer regiments, many of the 71st N. I. and on their bodies were found many leave certificates, above forty in number." (The Lucknow Guide).

Lucknow Terrace.

Also known as Chouper Stables, is so-called from the four arms of a cross in which form the block was orinally built. This building was erected by Sa'adat Ali Khan (1798-1814), who kept therein his most valuable horses. After the annexation of Oudh, it was converted into barracks for the 32nd Regiment. After the mutiny the arms east and west were demolished, converting the main portion of the building into apartments which are now let to private families at a moderate rent. The south end rooms are occupied by the Union Club, which is chiefly supported by the uncovenanted Service.

The road to the east of the building, which is called Outram road, was the route taken by General Havelock's relieving force to the Residency. Its continuation along the west line of Government House and the Canal is called after General Havelock.

Alum Bagh.

It is a walled enclosure on the Cawnpore road about two miles south-west of the Railway station. The edifice, in the centre of the garden, was built by one of Wajid Ali Shah's Begums. It was captured by General Havelock on the 25th September 1857, and the wounded and sick, with spare stores, were left here on the General's advance to the relief of the Residency. General Havelock is burried within the enclosure, on the north side of the building, which is, at present, in a state of disrepair. An obelisk marks the spot where repose the mortal remains of Major General Sir Henry Havelock. A tablet has recently been added to this monument in memory of Sir Henry Havelock, who was killed by the Afridis on the 30th December 1897.

"Here in this park his sacred ashes lie,
No more a sweet and pleasant sylvan glade,
But now a waste of weeds and filthy wreck.
Where starveling cattle browse a scanty blade,
Where foul and fetid odors taint the air.
Here on his battle ground he lies forgot.
A weeping widow, not his country, raised,
The simple monument that marks the spot."

JOSEPH B. S. BOYLE.

The Chukker Wali Kothie.

The site of this building, situate about 300 yards to the east of the Pile Bridge (recently re-constructed), is a mere mound with traces of its foundations, all overgrown with surpat grass. In its neighbourhood are the new Cemetery, and the Mad House or Lunatic Asylum (now Government Training School) all on the opposite side of the river. "The enemy made a desperate stand here on the advance of the column for the final capture of the city. It was stormed and taken on the 8th of March 1858, by part of the column under command of Sir James Outram, consisting of the 1st Bengal Fusiliers and two companies of the 79th Highlanders. This was the key of the rebel position, it was carried in gallant style, and their strong line of entenchments, which had been constructed on the right bank of the Goomty, was thereby turned, of which success the skirmishers on the opposite side of the river were apprised of by Lieut. Butler of the Bengal Fusiliers, who swam across the Goomty, and climbing the parapet entrenchment, remained exposed to a heavy fire until the work was occupied. After the occupation of the Chukkur Kothi the enemy were driven rapidly through the old Irregular Cavalry lines and suburbs to the Badshah Bagh. The fortified gates of this strong walled enclosure were blown open by our troops, who dashed in and captured the place, taking two guns."

THE GUIDE TO LUCKNOW.

Talkatora Karbala.

This is a grêat ground, for meeting of nearly all the Moharrum processions from the city for the final disposal of their tazias. On the occasion the approaches are crowded all round, and the several bands of the faithful have a hot and dusty day's work of it in forcing a passage, with more fightings within than without, under the coercive measures of City Police. Adjoining the Karbala, which is appropriated for burial purposes, is the Imambara of Malka Zamani, mother-in-law of Nassir-ud-din Haider. But since the last four or five years, owing to religious dispute the burial places of Tazias have been separated, the Sunnis burying their Tazias in Phul Katora and the Shias in Talkatora as usual.

KAZMINES.

These Kazmines are westward from the Chowk and are two in number. One, which is built by Sharf-ul-dowlah, is said to be a copy of the tombs of the two Imams, Moosa Kazim and Imam Kazim of Khorasan, and the other is built by Dianat-ul-dowlah on the model of the tomb of Imam Hussain, at Karbala. Except on the occasion of illuminations therein during the first ten days of Moharram, there is nothing to repay a visit.

THE DURGAH OF HUZRUT ABBAS.

This place of sanctity and resort, which is visited by Mohomedans on every Thursday, is said to contain the banner of Hazrat Abbas a relative of Hazrat Ali, who was killed in the battle of Karbala.

MURIAON.

Or Old Cantonments situate about two miles to the north of Badshah Bagh. Here the mutiny broke out on the 30th of May 1857. "A sepoy of the 30th N. I. reported at head-quarters that a mutiny would take place on that night, but apparently the information was discredited, for no intimation of it was sent to the Residency. The evening gun fired at nine o'clock and very soon after a few shots were heard and then one or more volleys of musketry, followed by two discharges of cannon. Presently the lurid glare from different quarters of the Cantonments announced that the bungalows had been fired. The leaders in this outbreak were the 71st N. I. and some of the 7th Light Cavalry. But the rebels were met by prompt and decisive measures on the part of the local government, and the tragic issues which followed elsewhere were here averted." (LUCKNOW GUIDE.)

CHAR BAGH.

This garden, situated in the neighbourhood of the Railway station has become noteworthy from an incident in the Indian mutiny. "The two Brigades under Generals Outram and Havelock of the relieving force met here on the 25th of September 1857.

The bridge, crossing the canal, was defended by a robel battery of four guns, including one or more heavy ones, and the houses close by were loopholed and full of riflemen and musketeers. For awhile Maudes Light Field Battery posted on the road endeavoured to silence the enemy's guns; but after a number of his gunners had fallen, the Infantry were put forward. A portion of the west Brigade lining the bank of the Char Bagh, which skirts the right side of the canal, poured a heavy fire of Enfields on the enemy's gunners, while the battery itself was most gallantly stormed and taken by the 1st Madras Fusiliers, supported by the 5th Fusiliers, led on by Captain H. M. Havelock, and Colonel B. Fraser Tytler. During the passage of the baggage, which occupied more than two hours, the entrance of the main street was held by the 78th Highlanders, who suffered severely in charging and taking two guns brought to bear on them by the rebels from the city side." (LUCKNOW GUIDE).

Fortress of Jellalabad.

The fortress of Jellalabad, now a heap of ruins, is a work of great antiquity. Natives report that it was built by Shuja-ul-dowlah after his defeat by the British at Buxar, a battle at which place was fought on the 23rd October, 1764, under the command of Major Munro.

The fortress is situate to the east of the Cawnpore Road. It was the extreme right of General Outram's position, and used as a store-depot. The garrison consisted of 150 infantry, 20 military train, 2 guns, and 20 Artillery men. The fort is almost surrounded by lakes aad marshes, from which the markets of Lucknow are supplied with wild fowl.

MOHURRUM.

"The term signifies most sacred, and is applied to a fast and solemn mourning, which commences on the evening of the new moon in the first month (Mohurrum.) It lasts, including the Ziyarat or visiting the grave, till the 12th. But the fast is kept for ten days, and called Ashura, from the Arabic signifying ten; houses are set apart for the mourning ceremonies and are called Ashur-khana, that is, "ten days' Taziah-khana, or "house of lamentation"; and Astanah "threshold" or Fakir's residence." In these places the tazias are exhibited during the whole period of the fast, whilst singers are engaged in dirges for the occasion. The moment, the new moon is seen, which is announced by beat of drum by watchmen, a spade is stuck into the earth, where a pit is dug two or three days after for a bonfire. At night men dance round the fires, fencing with swords and springing through and into the flames with cries of Alli Shah Hassein! Shah Hassein Duhla! &c., The Imambara, which is often also a mausoleum, as at Hosseinabad and elsewhere is substituted for the A'shurkhana by kings and courtiers and the wealthy. Here verses are chanted in honor of Hussein and Hussun, in memory of whom the fast is held. They were the sons of Ali, the cousin, and Fatimah his wife, the daughter of Mohomed (God may be pleased with all of them). Of these two brothers, the elder Hussein was poisoned by Yezid, the son of Mawiah, and the younger, Hussein, was murdered with all his retinue at Kabala in Turkish Arabia, in the 46th year of the Hejira: Zain-ul-Abideen, the eldest son of Hejira, alone escaped. On the night of the 7th a representation is exhibited of Burak, the horse or mule on which Mohomed ascended to heaven. On the 10th a bier called tazia, gaily decorated and lighted up, is carried in procession, and finally disposed of at the Kurbala. During these processions the most furious encounters take place between different parties, it being a point of honor not to give way, whilst an extra body of police are deputed to act in the same indomitable spirit. And with uproarious demonstration of frantic grief, and sundry attempts of violence and perhaps vengeance, amid the din of discordant trumpets, and the beating of divers drums, the tinkling of many cymbols, and the confusion of more tongues, the whole affair subsides with the dispersion of the crowds for another twelfth lunation.

The Mohurrum is strictly observed by the Shiahs chiefly, one of the two great sects of Mahomedans, the other being the Sunnies, so-called from their acceptance of the Sunna, or tradition of Mahomed, as a supplement to the Koran, and of almost equal authoritly whilst the *Shiahs* reject it. The former sect includes the Arabs, Turks, Afghans and Rohillas, and the latter, the Persians, and a great part of the people of Oudh and other parts of India." (LUCKNOW GUIDE.

Bridges of Goomti.

The Iron Bridge.—This elegant iron bridge, brought out from England in 1816 by order of Ghazi-ud-din Haider, consists of three segmental arches each formed of several parallel plates of iron, which are placed like girders from pier to pier. The king dying before its arrival, his son, Nasir-ud-din Haider, directed the bridge to be constructed in front of the Residency just where a small temple and ghat stood on the opposite side of the river. He gave the contract for erecting it to his own Engineer, a Mr. Sinclair, who commenced sinkings well in order to found piers, but could not succeed and the king died. The completion was however, delayed till Mohomed Ali Shah (1837—1842) the next king, took up the project and placed the same in the position in which it now stands.

The Pucca Bridge.—Also called Stone Bridge is not built of stone as is commonly called, but of pucca masonry. It is situate near the Muchhee Bhawan. It is of such a substantial structure as to outlast many a similar one of the present time and consists of thirteen arches out of which the central one is the largest and highest, in the rest, on both sides, are proportionately reduced, forming the roadway an uncommonly steep gradient from the centre to the extremeties either way. It was commenced by Munsur Ali Khan and completed by his grandson, Asuf-ud-dowlah, about the year 1780. It being considered unsafe, it has lately been rebuilt.

The Bruce's Bridge.— This bridge which marks it of recent construction, and marks the period of British occupation after the mutiny, consists principally of three segmental arches like the Iron Bridge, and is ornamented with ashlar in the exterier. It crosses the river opposite the Kaiser Bagh, connecting the Kursi road, a much frequented thoroughfare, with this important centre of the city.

The Pile Bridge.—This was also of recent construction connecting the Secunder Bagh, with the opposite quarter, where are the Lunatic Asylum or Mad house, and the new Cemetery. It fell down by the flood which continued so dangerously during the first week of October 1891, that hundreds of villages were drowned and lives end angered. It has now been rebuilt at the expense partly paid by the Government and partly by the Municipality of Lucknow.

LUCKNOW BAZARS.

—:0:—

In Lucknow there are numerous bazars or markets connected one each other, out of which a few are described below for the information of the visitors:—

CHOWK.—This was built in the time of Asuf-ud-daulah, but of the two gates at each end of it, the southern one is said to belong to an earlier date. It is called the Akbari Darwaza, and native report goes that Akbershah himself passed through Lucknow on his way to Nepaul, and after reducing to Raja of

Nepal to submission, returned through Lucknow again and set up this gate. This story is not supported by history, and is for many reasons unlikely. A more likely story is that one of the subadars of Oudh, built this gate and named it after Akbar, the founder of this subah. This is a very grand bazar throughout the whole city, where articles of every description are sold at the shops which are established at both sides of the road. Here almost all the shops are double-storied built with pucca bricks; the upper stories are occupied by the dancing girls and the lower story by shop-keepers. The road of this Chowk is so narrow as not to admit of two carriages abreast, therefore another Chowk has been recenty built and called New Chowk.

NEW CHOWK.—It lies to the left side of the old Chowk entering by the Akbari Darwaza a little higher ascending over the Farangi Mahal or (British Palace) Bridge. It has a wide metalled road, the shops being both sides, erected with pucca bricks but is not so populated as the old Chowk above described. Only a few shops of cloth merchants and others are there, to which people have to attend on requisition.

YEHYAGANJ.—Term *ganj* signifies to the market where grain is sold and Yehya Khan is the name of a wealthy man by whom it is said to be founded and hence so-called. Here copper basins and iron pots are sold and there are a few other shops of different trades for the requisites of those who live close to it.

NAKAS.--This is situated between Chowk and Yehyaganj. Here worn clothes, old pieces of irons, crockery, ponies and birds are sold. This market is generally attended by the people in the morning and evening only.

AMINABAD.—This was built by Amin-un-daulah and is next to Chowk in population. It has a very wide road surrounded both sides with pucca built shops of various trades and professions and is at all times of the day open for the public. Some portion of this market has been demolished and replaced by a park hereinafter mentioned.

HAZRATGUNJ.—Here, there are the shops of English Firms, such as Murray & Co., Whiteaway Laidlaw & Co., etc. etc., and Railway Offices at one side of the road. Opposite to the Post Office, on a small piece of land there is a *Ganj* where grain is sold and in the front part of this bazar, a garden has been beautifully laid out recently, here also a Kothwali to be called Hazratganj Police Station has lately been built by the Government.

NEW BUILDINGS AT LUCKNOW.

Since the publication of the last edition of this book considerable changes have been made in Lucknow. New roads and buildings of note have been constructed and the old native houses have been demolished and their sites have been sold to wealthy people, who have built houses in accordance with the Municipal orders and plans. The natives to whom the houses belonged, have been compensated by the Government for their loss.

The plan does credit to the idea as the place has become a great deal more sanitary and pleasant to look at.

A description with a brief account of different places are given below for the information and guidance of the visitors to Lucknow.

Hazrutganj Police Station.—The Principal Police Office is a large double storied place recently built to cope with the demand on the force, which has become considerably great. It has a European Inspector attached to it and stands in the centre of a square on which were formerly delapidated and squalid looking native shops, now raised to the ground. Around this have been built large and commodius double storied buildings by Rajah Tassaduq Rasul Khan of

Jhanagirabad and engineered by Mr. Lebanti, the contracting Engineer whose Marble and Cement Works meets the eye of the visitors *en route* Railway Station to their Hotel on the left of the road immediately after passing the Canal.

Canning College.—This was originally a building to the north side of Kaisar Bagh near the tomb of Saadat Ali Khan and his wife, now given over to the use of the Museum. This College has now been transferred to a range of buildings on the other side of the river Goomti almost opposite the Chuttur Munzil, in a place called Badshah Bagh. The College has been built on a very much grander scale to meet the increase of students and to permit of them taking in Boarders. Egress to it is from Bruce's Bridge *alias* Monkey Bridge.

McConaghy Free School.—This building has been erected with a view to enable the poorer classes of Europeans and Eurasians to send their children for education. It instructs the students both in mental and physical science having a *kindargarten* system attached to it, and with a staff of seven lady teachers. It also gives to children, whose parents cannot afford, clothes and boots. It is a medium sized building standing on a land of two bighas on Cantonment Road close by the Civil and

Military Hotel, South West of it conveniently placed near the habitations of the poor European and Eurasion community.

Medical College.—A large piece of land about 14 bighas selected for the purpose of erecting a building for a Medical College, on the same principle as the one in Calcutta, Lahore and Madras. Situated between Machi Bhawan, Victoria Park and Lady Kiniard's Hospital, it is quite close to the Banks of the Goomti. A range of buildings big and small in a nice and open spot. It is proposed to admit students both male and female of all denominations caste and creed. This is a very imposing structure, and will be the'means of the poorer classes of European and Eurasians having a place to lay up in, when they are ill; for at the present time there is no proper place. It will also be the means of making Lucknow more prominent.

Victoria Park.—A large piece of land very tastefully laid out with flower, fruit and vegetable trees and broad drives of red concret well beaten down, in it stands the famous clock tower, the clock of which gave so much trouble to set aright, after several tries by Engineers etc. it was put up by a Mechanic of the Oudh and Rohilkhand Railway named Mr.Mutloe, now dead. There is also a picture gallery in this park with the likenesses of the different Kings of Oudh hanging, and here also the office of the trustees of the Hussainabad trust is situated. The garden is so extensive that it has a separate water pumping station with a European Engineer and native assistant attached to it. It is situated between Chowk (Goal Darwaza), Nawab of Shees Mahal place Machi Bhawan (old fort) and the Medical College.

Aminabad Park.— A Market place where all kinds of imported, both English and foreign goods are sold along with country manufacture also. The different Banks have a branch in it also, and there is a branch post office. It has derived its name through the ground on which it stands, being a portion of Aminabad bazaar, the old houses having been demolished and new shops erected on a more elaborate style in a quadrangle of 3 sides with a lawn thrown out in the centre. This is light up by Kiston lights, has a fountain and a clock tower. The entrance being from all sides. This has also added to the thinning of the population, making it more sanitory and thus staving off a deal of sickness which year by year would otherwise have come about. This along with other places mentioned hereafter was planned out by Mr. Butler one of our most energetic Deputy Commissioners who has since received a promotion and gone to the

Government of India as Seceretery to Government Foreign office.

Meat Market, styled Saunder's Market.— An entire new building erected at the junction of La Touche, Cantonment, Circular and Banks road. It is a single storied place of large dimensions with gauze wire netting doors to keep out the flies, this is another of Mr. Butler's conceptions and is a very striking edifice, in it are marble slabs to help the butchers keeping the place clean. It has several skylights to it, allowing plenty of fresh air to get in, there are 4 entrances to it and it has a Bazaar Sergeant to see that the place is kept clean and in order. The Market opened with a garden party under the auspicious of H. H. Sir James Prescott Hewett L. G. of the U. P. of A. and Oudh and the elite of the station and has been styled Saunder's Market; all the other shops have been abolished and only the market will be used as the place for sale of both beef and mutton along with fish.

Shees Mahal.-(Palace of Glass) Dowlat Khana, a building now in ruins occupied by the richest Mohamedan, a Nawab in the service of the late King of Oudh, formerly built of glass, a portion of it has been re-erected by him with masonry. It has a large tank where some millions of rupees are supposed to have been thrown in, in a large iron safe.

La Touche Road.—This is one of the broadest roads in this station. It begins from the South gate of the Kaisar Bagh at the junction of Circular, Banks and Aminabad Roads goes through Nyagaon, Aminabad, bisecting Hewett, Abbott and Good Shed Roads and leads into the Oudh and Rohilkand Railway Station Charbagh and terminates there. There are buildings all along on both sides of the road erected for the purpose of shops and dwelling houses. This road was named after the late Lieutenant Governor of the United Provinces of Agra and Oudh, Sir James Digges La Touche; the object of the opening of the road was to make it convenient for the residents around Kaisar Bagh and its precincts, and also to thin the population of Aminabad which was very thickly peopled. It is largely patronised by all, especially in the evenings. It enables one to have a pleasant drive without quite tiring the horses or going through a crowded bazaar.

Hewett Road.—Another broad road, though not quite as broad as the above, makes its start from the Junction of Abbott and Railway Station Road bisecting La Touche, Aminabad and Canning Roads going through Fatehgange, Doulat Bagh and terminating a little beyond Saadutgunj. This with other roads have been opened with the object of making Aminabad healthy.

A GUIDE TO LUCKNOW.

Mall Road.—This is one of the longest, best kept and most frequented roads passing through Hazratgange, where all the European and large native merchants have their shops. It makes its start near Hussainabad Imambara, goes along by the side of the Residency, between the public Courts and Chutter Manzil (United Service Club) through Hazrutgange, passes by the Roman Catholic and Christ Churches (Protestant) the Exchange Cottage another range of buildings where large European and native shops are, then by Goverment House North Gate, over Canal, by the Loretto Convent through Cantonments and finally ends at the Race Course, a distance of 6 to 7 miles.

Walli Qudr Road.—Another broad Road opened for the convenience of people living East side of Kaisarbagh to reach the Municipal and City Magistrate Office, formerly the Military Prison, but owing to the distance it stands from Cantonments was given up to the Norman School and has now become the Courts of the City and the Bench of Hont Magistrates and the Municipal Offices both Civil and Enginering Departments; starting from Banks Road and ending at China Bazaar gate.

New Havelock Road.-A road of considerable width opened out with a view to enable residents living on the west of Canal to get to Cantonments by a more direct route, as well as with the object of making that part of the Station which had a village there very thickly populated sanitary; this is another short road covering a distance of only ¼th of a mile, it starts from Havelock road and ends at the Mall near the Loretto Convent and the General's Kothi.

Fountains.

There are several fountains presented by different people, that have been erected, these have greatly added to the beauty of the place and the donors daily receive unknown to themselves, great praise and thanksgiving.

No.—1 On a triangular piece of land between the Civil Dispensary, Allahabad Bank, Christ Church and the Exchange Cottages, Hazratgunge, has been presented by Babu Govind Pershad Bhargava, who also has a Iron Workshop, Machine Printing and Litho. Presses and Ice Factory.

No.—2 There, on a traingular piece of land between the Bank of Bengal, Kankar Walli Kothi and Raja of Jhangirabad's Town house, these are said to have been presented by the Hon'ble Raja Tassuduq Rassul Khan of Jhangirabad.

No 3.—Opposite Northgate Kaisar Bagh between China Bazaar Gate, the late Queen's Statue, Bruce's Bridge and Neil's gate. This fountain was presented to the public by the Hon'ble Munshi Madho Lall of Benares.

No 4.—On a triangular piece of land in Lall Bagh where public sports are held *e.g.* Cricket, Football and where Circuses and Theatrical Companies performing under tents hold their shows. It is between Isabella Thoburn College, Methodist Church, Amjad Ali Shah's Mukbara and Mission Road. This fountain was presented to the public by Pundit Jagpal Krishna, 1907.

No. 5.—Another fountain on a piece of land opposite the Deputy Commissioner's Court (*Roshun daula ke kacheri)* between the Courts and Kaisar Bagh, was erected by Khan Bahadar H. S. Shaban Ali Khan, Raja of Salempur.

No. 6.—This fountain is erected by Mahant Sant Ram Dass, to the memory of the late Mahant Harcharan Das Taluqdar, Miswasi, District Unao, this is a beautiful structure standing on a base of 100 feet cirumference at the head of Aminabad; where Banks Road bisects Cantonment, La Touche, Aminabad, Circular and Kaisar Bagh Roads, around it are, placed benches for visitors to sit, on this spot; there stood a very old Peepul tree and a place of Hindu worship, the latter has removed to a distance of 100 feet closer into the walls of the Kaisar Bagh, and the gate that was there standing and leading into Kaisar Bagh has been levelled to the ground.

—— :o: ——